DARK ROSE

Organized Crime and Corruption in Portland

ROBERT C. DONNELLY

DARK
ROSE

Organized Crime and Corruption in Portland

UNIVERSITY OF WASHINGTON PRESS
Seattle and London

UNIVERSITY OF WASHINGTON PRESS
PO Box 50096
Seattle, WA 98145–5096, USA
www.washington.edu/uwpress

LIBRARY OF CONGRESS CATALOGING-IN-PUBLICATION DATA
Donnelly, Robert C.
Dark rose : organized crime and corruption in Portland / Robert C. Donnelly.
    p. cm.
Includes bibliographical references and index.
ISBN 978-0-295-99111-5 (pbk. : alk. paper)
1. Organized crime—Oregon—Portland—History.
2. Corruption—Oregon—Portland—History.
3. Portland (Or.)—History.
I. Title.
HV6452.07D66 2011
364.1'060979549—dc22   2011000187

The paper used in this publication is acid-free and 90 percent recycled from
at least 50 percent post-consumer waste. It meets the minimum requirements
of American National Standard for Information Sciences—Permanence of Paper
for Printed Library Materials, ANSI Z39.48–1984.

FRONTISPIECE
Portland, Oregon. Acme Commercial Photographers, 1923. Library of Congress
Prints and Photographs Division, US GEOG – Oregon no. 42 (SOS).

CONTENTS

FOREWORD

Portland Has Not Always Been Portland

SURE, THE NAME'S BEEN THE SAME SINCE 1845, BUT THE twenty-first century city represents a radical break from the majority of its history.

Portland today has a worldwide reputation as a "capital of good planning," a place where concerned citizens work together to craft a city that not only works in the present but has the potential to survive the environmental challenges of the coming decades. It is the only city in the United States with a directly elected regional government and the first large metropolitan area to utilize an urban growth boundary to contain sprawl. It is a leader in new rail transit and bicycle commuting. It has built a vibrant downtown, recycled older neighborhoods, and enhanced natural areas within the city. It strikes many visitors as one of the most European of American cities—definitely a compliment when the visitor is from Europe.

Read a little history, however, and a very different city emerges. Portland in its first century was a frontier settlement, then a workingman's town, and then a rough-and-ready city with close ties to the farms and forests whose bounty stoked the economy. Businessmen ran the city in the interests of economic growth and real estate profits. Intellectuals couldn't wait to get out—people like John Reed at the start of the twentieth century and Gary Snyder at mid-century.

Portland's skid road was one of the largest in the country. Stretching for twenty-five blocks along the downtown waterfront was a district of cheap hotels, saloons, missions, flophouses, labor exchanges, and second-hand stores that served the needs of single male workers. Men, whose chief asset was their muscles, worked half the year repairing railroads, tending and harvesting crops, cutting and milling trees, crewing sailing ships, and building the cities and towns of the Pacific Northwest. In the off season they gravitated to the Portland waterfront to winter over, spending their money on food, drink, cards, and women. Immigrants from Italy, China, Greece, and Japan mixed with the native born. Those who could vote supported the Republican Party's political machine in the standard style of corrupt boss politics.

To be sure, there were efforts at both respectability and reform (they weren't exactly the same thing). Members of the elite culti-vated eastern manners and connections. They sent their children to Ivy League schools and erected offices and homes and civic buildings in proper Romanesque and Georgian revival styles. They staged a successful world's fair in 1905 to show off the city to visitors and laid the foundations of museums and parks. At the same time, members of the middle class could separate themselves from skid road and downtown vice by moving to new streetcar suburbs on the east side of the Willamette River. These were the folks who sup-ported Progressive reforms that included the adoption of the Com-mission form of government in 1913.

As Robert Donnelly shows, however, reform efforts did not crack the tight alliance among vice industries, politicians, police, and real estate owners. The Portland Vice Commission report of 1912 revealed the pervasiveness of gambling and prostitution in downtown Portland and embarrassed the powerful, but it made only a temporary dent in the problem of corruption. The city passed through the 1920s with murder and scandal over waterfront land development and the 1930s with labor strife that included an accidental potshot at Franklin Roosevelt's personal emissary.

The 1940s were even tenser, as 150,000 new residents crowded the city to build ships for the Allied war effort. Some of the workers brought their families, but many did not. Unattached young men needed outlets for their energy and their money. Movie theaters ran around the clock and brothels presumably did as well—pushed out of sight but not out of mind by government authorities. As Donnelly points out, the police regulated and contained vice rather than suppressing it. The mayor was notoriously on the take.

This is the context for Donnelly's story of the corruption scandals and Congressional investigations that rocked Portland in the 1950s. Vice industries were entrenched and law enforcement played along. Labor unions like the Teamsters were flush with members and led by men who saw opportunities to muscle in on profitable businesses. It took newspaper reporters and unwanted national publicity to show Portlanders what their city looked like to others.

What's striking about the history recounted in *Dark Rose* is that it marks the end of one Portland era and signals the beginning of another. The "progressive Portland" of today has its roots in the scandals of the 1950s, which discredited the old regime and put them on notice that there would be no more business as usual. Business and political leaders of the mid-1950s either adapted to change or saw their influence erode. The years from 1965 to 1975 would bring a veritable revolution to Portland politics, with new issues and new grassroots participants. Community activists made changes to the fabric of the city in ways that remade both downtown and neighborhoods and environmentalists, transportation advocates, and other new voices placed the city on a new trajectory of development that it is still following today.

Robert Donnelly has found a pivotal moment in Portland history. Nobody in the mid-1950s could have imagined the Portland of 2011, but their actions and inactions in those tumultuous years helped to clear the stage for the present-day city.

Carl Abbott
Portland State University

ACKNOWLEDGMENTS

I AM TRULY GRATEFUL FOR THE SUPPORT AND GUIDANCE FROM friends and family as I worked on *Dark Rose*. Like all great endeavors, I made a number of new friends while researching for this project, particularly Bob Larson, Arthur Kaplan, and Wally Turner. Wally and Arthur were both very generous with their time and provided valuable information and insight into a complicated period in Portland history. You will recognize Wally in the following pages; he was a great journalist and kindly shared with me his stories and life. Arthur had a long, distinguished legal career, highlighted by his work with Robert Kennedy and the McClellan Committee. Bob Larson thought of me and my research as he perused a neighborhood sale one weekend, and selflessly shared the small treasure he found. Portland writer Phil Stanford, while finishing his work on this topic, was also generous with his own insights, data, and time.

Several people were early readers of all or parts of this manuscript, each one of whom provided suggestions for improvement and encouragement to keep the project going. I would especially like to thank David Horowitz at Portland State University who supported my early research and read the earliest drafts. Having such a prolific writer review my work helped tremendously. My research would not have been completed without the support from faculty and friends at Marquette University, as well as funding from the Cyril E. Smith Family Fellowship and the Arthur J. Schmitt Fellowship. I would like to especially acknowledge Athan Theoharis, my great friend and mentor, and an incredible historian. It was truly a blessing to have him guide my research and writing at Marquette. I will always remember fondly the many dinners that Annmarie and I shared with Athan and Nancy during our time in Milwaukee.

The generous support of the William L. Davis S. J. Endowment at Gonzaga University helped this book to completion and my colleagues in the history department have been very patient and encouraging while I finished this project. I would especially like to thank Kevin O'Connor and Eric Cunningham, two respected historians, accomplished writers, and enthusiastic teachers, who took their valuable summer months to read an early draft of this work. Robert Carriker, another Gonzaga professor, also read the manuscript. I have tremendous respect for Bob and his accomplishments, and I am very fortunate that he kindly and generously shares his research, writing, and publishing expertise with young historians.

Behind every good writer is an editor and I am very lucky to have found Julie Van Pelt so early in the game. This work would not have been published without Julie's hard work, experience, and patience. I owe credit to the anonymous reader who the University of Washington Press chose to review the manuscript. The reader had faith in the project and each revision moved the book forward. I also recognize the Press and their willingness to gamble on a new author with a controversial topic. Julidta Tarver started the ball rolling; I sincerely appreciate her early interest and support. The editors and staff at UW Press are wonderfully enthusiastic about their work, and with each suggestion from editorial, marketing, and design, this book keeps getting better. Kathleen Pike Jones has been very patient and did an incredible job fixing my rookie mistakes. Marianne Keddington-Lang is clearly my guardian angel. She is a great friend and I cannot thank her enough for believing in me and this project. I know she is just as happy (and relieved) as I am to see my work here published. Thank you, Marianne.

My family, also, deserves great thanks. The Donnellys, Hoffmans, and Dorns have supported me faithfully and spiritually. My grandmother, Dorothy, told me often that if I work hard, anything is possible. She was a proud grandmother, she often said; I miss her deeply. I would like to also acknowledge Finnegan and Declan. I love my boys and their restless energy.

But, the greatest debt I owe is to Annmarie. She compromised her goals for mine and made sacrifices without hesitation. She is truly a partner in this endeavor; this project is as much her achievement as it is mine. I dedicate my first book to her.

DARK ROSE

Organized Crime and Corruption in Portland

INTRODUCTION

IN APRIL 1956, PORTLAND *OREGONIAN* INVESTIGATIVE REPORT-
ers Wallace Turner and William Lambert—using information
provided by the city's infamous crime boss, James B. Elkins—
exposed the city's organized crime rackets and the corrupt city law
enforcement officials who either tolerated or profited from them.
Most damning, the *Oregonian* reporters unwrapped a scheme by
Teamsters union officials to take over alcohol sales and distribution,
and profit from the city's vice rackets: prostitution, gambling, and
bootlegging.[1] The alarmed public outcry that followed revealed that
Portlanders were surprised by the collapse of civic virtue in their
officials, but scandals of this nature were by no means unique to
the Rose City—if anything, the sensational vice crimes of Portland
seemed to conform to a fairly commonplace pattern of nationwide
urban corruption in the post–World War II era.

Government officials, likewise, had been concerned for some
years about union racketeering. The Federal Bureau of Investigation (FBI) and the U.S. Senate had been gathering evidence on the
questionable organizational tactics of local Teamsters' bosses, to say
nothing of the flamboyantly illegal activities of its most prominent

leaders. Reports of labor racketeering from Portland and around the country inspired powerful leaders in the U.S. Senate, particularly Democratic Senator John McClellan and his Chief Counsel Robert Kennedy, to investigate racketeering by union officials in many U.S. cities. By 1957, the U.S. Senate Select Committee on Improper Activities in the Labor or Management Field, better known as the McClellan Committee, discovered that Portland experienced the same incidence of labor racketeering, organized crime, and political corruption as the larger cities of New York, Seattle, Chicago, Los Angeles, and Detroit. "Were it not that the conspirators in this particular case had a falling out," the McClellan Committee concluded in its 1958 interim report, "the Committee believes that gambling and law enforcement in Portland would now be completely under the domination of a Teamsters-backed underworld. In other cities of the United States, where similar tactics have been employed, this type of domination has been achieved successfully."[2] In fact, the Portland case was vital to the Senate investigation. Witnesses from the Pacific Northwest, including Turner, Lambert, and Elkins, opened the hearings in 1957 with explosive testimony of urban vice and labor racketeering that implicated national labor leaders and local law enforcement officials.

Portland's vice scene and its entanglement with labor racketeering made the city critical to investigating, if not unraveling, a national crime network. Federal investigators found that Teamsters Vice President Frank Brewster ordered union organizers to control liquor distribution in Oregon and then opened brothels, launched gambling operations, and managed bars and clubs to profit from Portland's lucrative vice industry. To do this, they bribed local and state law enforcement officials. *Time* magazine suggested that without the *Oregonian* exposé, the McClellan Committee's investigation would have been limited to the Teamsters union officials' abuse of union funds and would have had little evidence of collusion among union officials, organized crime, and law enforcement officers. The magazine further suggested that the *Oregonian* provided a public service by inspiring the Senate committee to expand its investigation, which ultimately uncovered evidence that Teamsters President Dave Beck embezzled union funds and that Teamsters Vice President Jimmy Hoffa was connected to the mob. *Time*'s editors characterized the *Oregonian* as a "comfortable, conservative newspaper that is normally inclined to sit back and rock on Portland's front porch," but acknowledged that the exposé was "tough and hazardous" reporting.[3]

The case in Portland demonstrated patterns of vice and corruption consistent with those present in larger U.S. cities and reveals a generally unknown, but truly fascinating element of the local history of a great American city. Among cities like Cleveland, Pittsburgh, Seattle, and Detroit, a pattern of municipal reform reveals itself. Looking at Portland's history and the recurrence of vice and law enforcement corruption enables further insight and understanding of the post–World War II city and the post–World War II period as a response to progressive reform. Portland itself is an exceptional case study of repeated and failed efforts by progressive reformers to clean up municipal government and police morality.

Progressive reformers attacked political, economic, and social problems in late nineteenth- and early twentieth-century America. Initially, they focused on the trusts and large corporations that seemingly monopolized the nation's economy. Breaking these monopolies would level the field for smaller businesses. Progressives fought for women's suffrage, social services for the poor, and further protection for laborers, especially women and children. They also waged an intense battle against prostitution between 1895 and 1920 when red-light districts and brothels were more visible than ever in the American city. Newspaper exposés in many cities were written about the "white slave" industry, while many popular books and movies depicted an international conspiracy to sell young girls into prostitution. In 1903, Congress amended the Immigration Act of 1875 to permit the deportation of immigrant prostitutes or any foreign-born citizen convicted of employing a prostitute. Congress also passed the Mann Act in 1910, making it a federal offense to transport women across state borders for "immoral purposes."[4] State and city organizations conducted their own investigations, and in several cities, including New York and Portland, convinced municipal officials to sponsor vice commissions to study prostitution, as well as gambling and drinking, to determine ways to combat the "social evils." The anti-vice crusades of the early twentieth century succeeded in closing down many urban red-light districts, but prostitutes, gambling parlors, and popular drinking establishments simply moved to other parts of these cities and flourished.

Many progressives blamed alcohol for many social problems— drinking took wages from poor families, spawned crime, contributed to domestic violence, and impeded industrial efficiency. Political reformers also associated saloons with urban politicians and powerful political machines, and believed that by attacking alcohol, they indirectly hurt the political boss—the corrupt party leader who gained political power and collected payoffs by granting special favors to local businessmen. Saloonkeepers, liquor dealers, and beer brewers contributed to the boss's campaigns; therefore, many politicians were tied financially to the city's vice industry. This was the case in New York, Boston, Chicago, and Portland. Protected by those officials who shared the profits, the vices flourished in early twentieth-century American cities.

In Portland, where the principal political leaders were associated with the railroads, utilities, and real estate, the political machine was led by bankers, lawyers, and developers who were connected to these industries necessary for the growth of any city. These men governed to benefit their private interests and those of their cronies.[5] The *Oregon Journal* editorialized in 1912, "It is the secret and silent gentlemen who buy automobiles and mansions from the tainted profits of the underworld that are the ramparts of the system. They are the bulwarks and framework that keep the terrible structure from falling. Theirs is the influence that joins with city governments, with city officials and city police in staying the hands that try to fumigate and cleanse. It is money, money, money that sustains and feeds the system."[6]

Another focus of progressive reformers, therefore, was corruption in municipal government. These reformers attacked the city boss and his special interests—saloons, brothels, and corporate interests with lucrative and proprietary city contracts. Historian Richard Hofstadter argues that progressives wanted to restore popular government, "as they imagined it to have existed in an earlier and purer age."[7] They attacked the political machine and advocated local government authority whose actions would be open to public scrutiny. Reformers in many cities gained ground by appealing to nativists, who saw bosses as representative of immigrant interests, and to social activists fighting for temperance and law enforcement. To the progressive, Hofstadter asserts, government was the responsibility of all citizens, as demonstrated in the temperance and vice crusades.[8]

In many cases, progressives celebrated the elections of reform mayors, such as Tom Johnson (1901–1909) in Cleveland, Samuel "Golden Rule" Jones (1897–1904) in Toledo, Hazen Pingree (1889–1896) in Detroit, and Harry Lane (1905–1909) in Portland, who challenged party bosses and tried to reform their local governments. Many political reformers lobbied state legislatures to enact electoral changes to help reform local government and solve social problems. The initiative and referendum processes were two important victories for reformers that gave voters more legislative power. Oregonians approved these legislative tools in 1902 and, by 1918, more than twenty other states had approved one or both of these reform proposals. Many states, likewise, initiated the direct primary, which was intended to undercut the political boss's power of appointing a party's electoral candidates. The recall, another progressive initiative, allowed voters to remove an elected official from office through a special election. The electorate in Oregon approved the direct primary in 1904 and the recall in 1908. Together these reforms were designed to make local and state governments more democratic and eliminate corruption.

Yet, progressive reformers were not always able to gain support for such sweeping changes. During the Progressive Era, many American cities witnessed a new definition of civic corruption as commercial profiteers entered the world of municipal vice. In Seattle, for example, reformers were continuously frustrated as voters during the Progressive Era, and even into the Depression years, selected mayors friendly with vice businessmen. According to Seattle historian Richard C. Berner, the city's "open town policy" was upheld by the relationship between the police department and those who promoted prostitution, gambling, and bootlegging. "Since these illegal practices were fairly common knowledge," Berner argues, "they could not have continued without police protection."[9] In fact, corruption and vice racketeering led to the murder of a young police chief in 1901, and subsequent reform efforts by mayors Richard Ballinger (1904–1906) and Bertha Landes (1926–1928) were unsuccessful. Political and social reformers in Seattle were no match for the stronghold that racketeers John Considine, Clarence Gerald, Roy Olmstead, and Gideon Tubber had on the city from 1900 to the 1940s.[10]

Historian Mark Haller's study of crime, criminal justice, and reform in Chicago from 1900 to 1930 offers revealing insights regarding the relationship between politicians, law enforcement officials, and organized criminals in the early twentieth-century city. In Chicago, as in many cities, criminal activity and the criminal justice system were rooted in the ethnic neighborhoods and provided a means of social mobility. Consequently, politicians, law enforcement officials, and criminals often shared similar experiences and social values.[11] Thus, these groups, because of their frequent contact, Haller explains, developed a variety of relationships and mutual obligations. In Portland, however, city officers and criminals did not share common ethnic backgrounds or social status. As a younger city built and maintained by third- or fourth-generation immigrants from the East Coast, Portland was a town of opportunists who had little regard for ethnic loyalty. Portland's politicians used government to further the interests of local utilities, real estate development, and the railroads.

In many cities, criminal activities and the relationships cultivated by law enforcement officials and criminals were dependent upon the location. Gambling, for example, was an accepted vice among certain groups and in certain neighborhoods in Portland. Prostitution during different periods in both Chicago and Portland was confined to one or more red-light districts. "Where such activities were accepted," Haller asserts, "the police were under little day-to-day pressure to enforce unpopular laws and, in fact, were under considerable pressure to develop informal relations that would maintain order rather than enforce the law."[12] Furthermore, due to an overburdened criminal justice organization, an informal system of law enforcement came to replace a formal system.[13] This proved to be the case in Portland from the early decades of the twentieth century until the post–World War II period, when the police bureau was overwhelmed with petty crime, car thefts, safecracking, and juvenile delinquency. Prostitution was eventually regulated and confined to certain areas, illegal gambling was monopolized by a small handful of racketeers who bribed police officers, while bootlegging—serving liquor in unlicensed clubs or distributing liquor without a license before and after Prohibition—was targeted primarily by state officials.

The relationship between organized crime figures and corrupt police officials was first publicly exposed in 1885 in New York City. According to New York's Lexow Commission, brothels, gambling dens, pool halls, and other vice establishments operated without any attempt to conceal their activities in spite of city ordinances making these activities illegal. In fact, the commission concluded that the city's police regulated and controlled vice. The commission discovered that during the depression of 1893–94, many New York City police officers were bribed with diamonds, which had retained their value during the economic slump.[14]

In 1950, the highly publicized hearings of the Kefauver Committee—the U.S. Senate Special Committee on Organized Crime and Interstate Commerce—revealed that the relationship between organized crime figures and corrupt city officials continued. The investigation inspired public revulsion toward organized crime and eventually linked mafia figures to corrupt politicians. Focusing on police corruption in Philadelphia, New York, Chicago, Los Angeles, and other cities, Senator Estes Kefauver and his investigators found that organized criminal syndicates controlled the vice rackets and the political machinery in many of the country's larger cities, and conducted operations similar to those of the political machines of the Progressive Era.

The Kefauver Committee hearings heard the testimonies of more than six hundred witnesses in fourteen cities over fifteen months. In New York, over fifty witnesses described the criminal, political, social, and legal activities of the nation's largest crime syndicate, which was headed by Frank Costello, the boss of the New York County gambling rackets and controller of the Democratic Party organization. This syndicate, created by Lucky Luciano in the 1930s and comprised of bootleggers, gamblers, and hitmen, developed close relationships with politicians. Allegations of municipal corruption eventually forced the mayor of New York City, William O'Dwyer, to resign. In Tampa, Florida, the Kefauver Committee exposed a conspiracy involving the sheriff of Hillsborough County who received payments for protecting gamblers. Senate investigators had also located a "bagman" in Philadelphia who carried payoffs of $3,000 to $4,000 per month to each of the city's thirty police districts.[15]

These cases are very similar to the case in Portland, where city leaders and law enforcement officers took bribes to ignore gambling, prostitution, and bootlegging. There was an elaborate system of tolerance in Portland during the 1940s that ultimately contributed to the city's economy. Mayor Earl Riley's administration (1941–1948) ignored the vice industry, especially those vice properties owned and managed by his friends and political supporters. Riley admitted that regulation rather than abatement of these properties was the best solution to Portland's vice-crime problem.

The City Club of Portland launched investigations in 1945 and 1947 of vice conditions in the Rose City. Subsequently, the club accused city officials of protecting vice operators "in consideration of a substantial 'payoff' to some police officers and public officials."[16] Club investigators concluded that a local organized crime syndicate controlled the vice rackets in Portland. Their evidence pointed to vice lord James Elkins, but he could not have controlled the city's vice industry if not for a coalition with law enforcement officers, city leaders, and labor union officials.

What makes the post–World War II period in Portland particularly interesting is the occurrence of labor racketeering. Labor unions, initially created to protect the laborer from the rapid growth of Big Business, ultimately, too, became susceptible to crime and corruption. Franklin Roosevelt's New Deal served to politicize the suffering of the American workers, and New Deal legislation recognized labor's right to organize and bargain collectively. The New Deal gave birth to Big Labor, and World War II and war production increased the membership rolls. In 1941, labor unions represented nearly nine million workers; by 1945, they had organized another six million. Organized labor was big and politically powerful. Nevertheless, the failure of the postwar bargaining system, the hostility to unions exhibited by management and corporations, the fragmentation and decentralized power of labor, and the relative vulnerability of the labor movement permitted union oligarchies to misappropriate union funds, devalue labor's political influence, and engage in criminal activity.[17] In 1954, labor leaders in Seattle and Portland attempted to organize Portland's vice industry the same way they had organized legitimate industries.

While historians have examined this phenomenon in detail as it occurred in older cities such as New York and Chicago, Portland's experience with organized crime, political corruption, and labor racketeering has been relatively unexplored. There exists a vast body of evidence that reveals the entanglement of Portland's criminals and law enforcement officials, especially during the post–World

War II period. According to FBI documents, McClellan Committee reports and transcripts, city and state law enforcement records, oral histories, and wiretap recordings, Portland was as riddled with vice crime in the postwar era as it was during the wild and woolly mid-nineteenth century when it was founded.

A challenge of researching law enforcement and political corruption is that the city and police officials involved, for obvious reasons, neither created nor maintained records of payments received, solicitations of bribes, or illegal contracts. Vice operators, too, are careful not to keep records of their nefarious dealings with police and corrupt politicians. This history of underworld Portland relies upon the memoirs and testimonies of criminals, including informants and insiders who would have been privy to confidential disclosures by criminals and public officials. The contentions made in these sources are often unverified, or, for that matter are unverifiable, but many claims are supported by more reliable sources.

The Turner-Lambert reports that exposed Portland's vice underworld follow the tradition of the turn-of-the-century muckrakers. The story caused such a fury that the reporters secretly moved out of the *Oregonian* headquarters and into a hotel to avoid the backlash. At the time, critics questioned the reporters' and the editors' motives for publishing the explosive story, saying it was speculation that relied on tainted or unknown sources—some sources were indeed individuals who had either an economic or political interest in seeing their rivals in the vice industry exposed. But the *Oregonian* reports have since been corroborated by FBI and congressional sources.

FBI records, obtained through the Freedom of Information Act, demonstrate how the Teamsters used political pressure and threats of violence to organize Portland's legitimate industries as well as the bootlegging, gambling, and prostitution rackets. Charged with a mission to monitor "subversive" activities in the 1930s, FBI agents began an intense surveillance of organized labor, and specifically the Teamsters in Portland and Seattle. The reports, collected and compiled in the 1950s by Special Agent in Charge (SAC) Joseph Santoiana Jr., provide insight into the Teamsters' role in organized crime, and show the degree to which Portland vice operators, politicians, and police also participated in illegal activities.

In the 1950s, a U.S. Senate investigation of labor racketeering offers further data on municipal corruption and vice crime in Portland. Robert Kennedy, chief counsel for the McClellan Committee, investigated the Teamsters' vice activities and documented the committee's findings in his book, *The Enemy Within*. His papers, which include notes, memos, and other documents related to the Portland case, are held at the John F. Kennedy Library in Boston. The McClellan Committee transcripts themselves are also extremely useful and informative, providing a detailed, if technical account of the committee proceedings. The hearing transcripts, which are available in government depositories, provide useful testimony, and Senator McClellan's papers, archived at Ouachita Baptist University, provide speeches, affidavits, and correspondence that describe the efforts to expose labor racketeering in Portland and other cities. This collection also contains a large "derogatory file," which holds hundreds of letters, many written by Oregonians, in response to the congressional hearings. Some were written by Northwest Teamsters who criticized the abuse union officials received during the McClellan Committee hearings.

These sources, as authentic and plentiful as they are, nevertheless, pose certain problems. First of all, because FBI agents obtained testimonies that did not result in prosecution, the evidence was not subject to the kind of test inherent in judicial proceedings—admissibility of evidence, such as hearsay and rumor, and the opportunity for defense attorneys to challenge the credibility of witnesses. Second, congressional hearings were not fact-finding investigations, but were intended to deliberately shape public opinion for a purpose, in this case, the enactment of labor-racketeering legislation. Senator McClellan had his own political agenda, as did the panelists, and the committee's chief counsel, Robert Kennedy. During the committee's hearings, the senators and staff counsel never challenged the testimony of "friendly" witnesses who were allowed to make unverified charges. At the same time, hostile witnesses were subject to questioning that attacked their integrity and, as a result, possibly created a false impression.

Although some of the charges seem overdrawn, these sources, when corroborated with other sources, provide a generally reliable account of Portland's vice scandal, political corruption, and lax policing. For example, interviews with former *Oregonian* reporter Wallace Turner, former U.S. Senate investigator Arthur Kaplan, and former U.S. Attorney Sidney Lezak offer valuable insight into law enforcement, crime, and corruption in postwar Portland. Without their personal recollections, a study such as this would be difficult and grossly incomplete. Moreover, wiretap and audio recordings of room conversations among certain Teamsters, local vice racketeers, and Multnomah County District Attorney William Langley provide further evidence of collusion. The King Tower tapes reveal Langley's whitewash of a grand jury investigation into graft in the Oregon Liquor Control Commission, and together with grand jury and McClellan Committee testimony, show that former Multnomah County sheriff and Portland Mayor Terry Schrunk allowed certain gambling operations to run in the city and surrounding areas.[18]

Yet, no study of Portland's past can ignore the important published works of Carl Abbott, E. Kimbark McColl, and Jewel Lansing. Abbott's *Portland: Planning, Politics, and Growth in a Twentieth-Century City* is the most comprehensive history of Portland's urban development and clearly explains the coalition of business and politics and its influence on the growth of the city. E. Kimbark MacColl has published three volumes on Portland's history: *The Shaping of a City* (1976), *The Growth of a City* (1979), and *Merchants, Money, and Power* (1988). Together they have made MacColl Portland's most cited source on the city's brief, yet colorful history. In each book, he frequently discussed corruption and vice crime in the Rose City; however, MacColl concludes his study of Portland at 1950. A more recent history, *Portland: People, Politics, and Power, 1851–2001*, by former city and county auditor Jewel Lansing, starts where MacColl left off.

This history is not the first to study vice crime and political corruption in Portland. In his 1981 PhD dissertation, Joseph Uris analyzed Portland's vice scandal of the 1950s through the use of sociological notions of functionalism and Marxist theories of capitalism. He also scrutinized the *Oregonian* newspaper and its main competitor, the *Oregon Journal*, while dissecting Portland's political machines and reform movements. Uris's work is a valuable sociological analysis of the relationship between crime, politics, and the community. Local journalist Phil Stanford offers *Portland Confidential: Sex, Crime, and Corruption in the Rose City*, a look at prostitution, gambling, and drug trafficking in the 1950s. Stanford is an incredible storyteller; his readers always want more.

Given the proliferation of novels and films that have popularized organized crime, no case of urban corruption seems extreme or extraordinary no matter how outrageous. Such corruption is arguably a by-product of the growth of American cities. The magnitude of the Portland vice scandal and its affect on national investigations proves that the city is worthy of greater study, if only to enlarge our understanding of Portland's development in the context of postwar urban history. What follows is the history of Portland's seedy side, particularly the vice scandal of 1956, revealing the "stench behind the roses."[19]

Southwest Broadway, downtown Portland, Oregon, ca. 1950.
Oregon Historical Society, OrHi 12695.

R. Earl Riley, n. d.
City of Portland Archives,
A2005-005.946.8.

James Elkins, 1958.
Oregon Historical Society, OrHi 104504.

Mayor Dorothy McCullough Lee,
1948. Courtesy of *The Oregonian*.

Thomas Maloney, 1957.
Courtesy of *The Oregonian*.

Joseph McLaughlin testifying
before the McClellan Committee, February 1957. Courtesy of
The Oregonian.

Multnomah County District Attorney William Langley, June 1956.
Photograph by Herb Alden. Courtesy of *The Oregonian*.

King Tower apartments, Portland, Oregon, 1950.
Oregon Historical Society, OrHi 104501.

Police Chief James Purcell with his top aides, January 1953.
Courtesy of *The Oregonian*.

Mayor Fred Peterson, 1953. Courtesy of *The Oregonian*.

James Elkins testifying before the McClellan Committee, March 1957.
Oregon Historical Society, OrHi, 106103.

Mayor Terry Schrunk testifying before the McClellan Committee, March 1957. Courtesy of *The Oregonian*.

Alleged conspirators in the selection of the Exposition-Recreation Center, August 1956. Courtesy of *The Oregonian*.

Oregonian reporters Wallace Turner (left) and William Lambert, c. 1956.
Courtesy of *The Oregonian*.

ONE

EARLY PORTLAND
AND THE FAILURE OF
PROGRESSIVE REFORM

IN THE EARLY DECADES OF THE NINETEENTH CENTURY, Portland was known simply as "The Clearing," a rest stop for those traveling between Fort Vancouver and Oregon City. In 1843, the town was founded, and a toss of the coin—a gamble—led to the site's naming in 1844. Massachusetts lawyer, Asa Lovejoy, and Francis Pettygrove, a businessman from Maine, shared the land, but could not agree on a name. Pettygrove won the coin toss, therefore, his beloved Portland, Maine, had a namesake on the West Coast. Portland, Oregon, was established before other notable northwestern cities, such as Seattle, Tacoma, or Boise, and quickly began to grow. The personality of this new town, which bulged with eight hundred people in 1850, was molded by a thriving commercial life that grew out of the abundant farmlands of the Willamette Valley and the thick forests of Oregon's Cascade and Coast mountain ranges. The city's wharves soon filled with lumber, wheat, and fruit, which were readied for shipment to distant markets. When the gold rush transformed San Francisco from a coastal hamlet into a boomtown in the 1850s, Portland provided the lumber to build the "City by the Bay." By the end of the nineteenth century, Portland, although not as glamorous as San Francisco or Denver, was an important city in the West.[1]

As Portland grew in the 1870s and 1880s, it became an important river city, like St. Louis and Cincinnati. Portland's character was shaped by a conservative financial community that pursued sound investments in both new business opportunities and old establishments; yet Portland's investors were not opposed to occasional risky speculation. Town leaders were committed to public education and sought to develop a unique, if fairly traditional, Portland culture, one that differed from the ethnic-flavored environment of Milwaukee and the loud boosterism of Chicago. According to historian E. Kimbark MacColl, "Portland's characteristics blended together to give the city a special quality of affluence, tempered by civility and good taste."[2] Portland's "particular sense of place," historian Carl Abbott explains, "is based on its everyday environment."[3] Portland's serene environment of wooded hilltops, majestic rivers, and nearby snow-covered peaks earned Portland the moniker, "Pearl of the Northwest."

The shining city on the hill also had a familiar underside. Like many American cities in the nineteenth century, Portland's gambling dens, brothels, and saloons boomed, the by-product of turbulent, expansionist, and lawless times. By 1864, the growing town included seven hundred transients in hotels and boardinghouses, and the presence of gold in the region, combined with land speculation and a boisterous waterfront, stimulated the construction of saloons, dancehalls, and brothels where men indulged in various "sinful" pleasures.[4] By the early 1880s, dozens of entrepreneurs profited from the lucrative enterprises of prostitution, gambling, and liquor, while the town's economic elite and municipal leaders owned and managed many of the properties linked to these activities. Since the middle- to upper-class—Portland's "establishment"—were responsible for civic governance, there was an obvious conflict between their moral and law enforcement duties and their unsavory side interests. Businessmen controlled Portland politics as well as the contracts for municipal services. The principal men of the city not only profited from railcar service, street paving and maintenance contracts, public utilities, and insurance policies, but also from the city's illegal operations. Given their social, political, and financial connections, they were disinclined to stifle the profitable gambling, liquor, and prostitution operations that reformers wanted to eliminate. This would remain true into the 1950s.

Before the Civil War, municipal corruption was less common in America's young cities than it was after the war. Antebellum urban populations were smaller and enterprising civic leaders had less incentive and fewer opportunities to capitalize on their positions. However, as cities grew after the war, opportunities for graft and illegal agreements increased as city officials created public services and signed lucrative contracts.[5]

In 1883, for example, Portland Mayor James Chapman publicly admitted that he had bought his 1882 election. He had agreed to appoint former City Councilman Lucerne Besser and acquaintance Tom Connell to top city jobs in exchange for their support. Financial duress, Mayor Chapman explained, motivated him to sign a contract with Besser in 1882, appointing Besser superintendent of streets and Connell chief of police in exchange for an immediate payment of $1,000, and $1,000 each year once he was elected.[6] Besser also agreed to use his influence with the Multnomah County legislative delegation to amend the city charter and increase the mayor's annual salary from $1,500 to $5,000. Unfortunately for Connell, the incumbent police chief, W. H. Watkins, had secured seven city council votes and was able to remain in office, thus denying Chapman the opportunity to honor the contract with Connell. After Mayor Chapman boldly confessed to the scheme, the city council impeached him. Chapman's defense betrayed the cynicism of opportunists everywhere. "You know that such bargains are made before every election," he volunteered. "Presidents of the United States do it too."[7]

"The politician," muckraker Lincoln Steffens warned in 1904, "is a businessman with a specialty."[8] Writing for *McClure's Magazine*, Steffens argued that corruption was the inevitable consequence of a society that holds power, wealth, and status as its most coveted prizes. "Politics is business. That's what's the matter with it."[9] Different cities, however, experienced cycles of corruption that grew out of their own historical development. Paving streets, adding sewer and water lines, and introducing public transportation required contracts that municipal leaders manipulated and distributed for financial and political gain.[10] At the same time, city dwellers—and, more important, city leaders—began to follow the newly constructed rail lines to the new suburbs, which had the effect of decentralizing the urban core. The Willamette River divided the old city from its burgeoning additions, where the middle and upper classes sought out lush parks and peaceful neighborhoods. By 1906, the population on the east side of the river surpassed the west side.[11] In 1910, three thousand houses were being built on the east side, while only 132 new houses were under construction west of the river. Civic leaders moved into the upper northwest, southwest, and eastern sections of the city and no longer viewed the crime problem in the city's core as their responsibility.[12]

This movement away from the urban core in American cities—compounded by an increase in crime, poor living conditions, and inadequate city services—opened the door for political machines and corrupt bosses. In Chicago, for example, Michael "Hinky Dink" Kenna and "Bathhouse John" Coughlin, two powerful political bosses of the city's First Ward, controlled Chicago's vice operations and used the criminal industry to fund elections and their vice connections to reward party faithful, including racketeers Johnny Torio and the young Al Capone. Tammany Hall controlled New York City politics throughout the nineteenth century through to the 1930s by increasingly drawing constituents from the city's burgeoning immigrant population, who in turn voted for the machine's bosses, such as William M. "Boss" Tweed. In eastern cities, many political bosses started out as saloonkeepers and shop owners with ties to specific ethnic communities. They typically worked their way up the political ladder by making promises—a job for a neighborhood boy or a city contract for a friend who could dig ditches. The political machine was the principle source of assistance for immigrants and other working class individuals. It was an organization, however, that did not propagate party principles; rather, it was interested in perpetuating the organization itself.[13] The vast profits earned by public utility franchises, the immensely lucrative public works contracts, and the seemingly unlimited municipal expenditures provided astounding opportunities for graft. "There is no denying," British writer James Lord Bryce concluded, "that the government of cities is the one conspicuous failure of the United States."[14]

In Portland, the interests of business were far more important than community interests. By the end of the nineteenth century, private interests—especially those connected to railroads, utilities, and real estate—exploited Portland. John Mitchell and Joe Simon, both experienced railroad lawyers, were Portland's answer to the political boss. While their domains were modest in size compared to New York's powerful Tammany Hall or George Cox's impressive organization in Cincinnati, Mitchell and Simon ruled the state's dominant Republican Party and controlled Portland's city hall and unabashedly exploited their ability to award local contracts and special favors.

Portlanders elected Mitchell to the state senate in 1862. Two years later, he was elected senate president and in 1872 was selected by the state legislature to serve in the U.S. Senate. He was a dominant force in Oregon Republican politics, but Mitchell's personal problems were common knowledge. He reportedly fathered several children with different women and entered into a bigamous marriage. He also devised a diabolical land scheme in 1869. The catalyst for the scheme was the death of Elizabeth Caruthers, heir to over 265 acres of land adjacent to the expanding city of Portland. She died without a will or any apparent beneficiary. Mitchell, with a few friends, found a man in St. Louis to pose as Joe Thomas, her former husband. The group arranged for his transportation to Portland, where he testified to his relationship with Elizabeth Caruthers and on this basis claimed the land. Mitchell and his partners paid the imposter and provided another $8,000 for a deed that granted them the coveted property rights. The schemers then formed the South Portland Real Estate Association and sold the land off in sections. They divided the money they made, with Mitchell receiving $10,000. Although Thomas's chicanery was exposed in 1873, the real estate transactions were never contested. Portland Mayor Bernard Goldsmith had received a $20,000 kickback, and John Mitchell had already been chosen to represent Oregon in the U.S. Senate.[15]

Mitchell's political cronies shared their leader's unscrupulous professional ethics. Jonathan Bourne, a wealthy and eccentric socialite, admitted to a friend in Washington, D.C., that he had spent $10,000 to stuff ballot boxes for Mitchell's Republican allies in 1896. Bourne had also used a $225,000 contribution from the Southern Pacific Railroad to elect sixty representatives to the U.S. House of Representatives; before receiving the money, the shameless recipients of this aid signed pledges of loyalty. According to Bourne, the definition of an honorable man was not only one that he could buy, but one "who would stay bought, and who would maintain his silence."[16]

During the 1896 presidential campaign, the Mitchell machine and pro-silver Republicans supported the Democratic candidate, William Jennings Bryan.[17] Allegedly, Bourne wired the notorious Billy Smith, a criminal in California and a known supplier of election repeaters, the men hired to vote over and over again for a candidate. In return for their votes for Bryan in Oregon, Bourne agreed to pay the repeaters' transportation and living costs. Smith agreed to supply the men on the condition that Bourne would find a way to persuade Portland law enforcement officials to remove his picture from the "most wanted" wall in the police station. With the deal sealed, Bourne and Smith were seen at the Arlington Club the night after the presidential election burning the photo that hung on the wall. Meanwhile, their opponents in the McKinley camp, led by influential Portlander Henry Corbett, were stuffing ballot boxes in towns up and down the Willamette River. It was later revealed that repeaters accounted for nearly six thousand votes, more than enough to influence the outcome of the election. Bourne later admitted that "with an honest vote Oregon would have gone for Bryan by 4,000."[18] McKinley secured Oregon by a little more than two thousand votes.

Although Mitchell lost some battles, he served several terms in the U.S. Senate. Late in his career, however, he was caught in a shady land deal that ultimately crippled his influence. To prevent large operators from controlling all of the land in the West, the U.S. Congress passed the Timber and Stone Act in 1878, which allowed land grants to courageous homesteaders who promised to live on the land. In 1904, rumors of abuse of the act were so pervasive that the federal government appointed a special prosecutor, Francis Heney, to investigate. The charges were that Stephen A. D. Puter and other lumber barons had hired claimants to purchase individual plots that they then sold to timber companies. The scheme allowed timber companies to collect large tracts of land set aside for farmers and homesteaders. "Thousands upon thousands of acres, which included the very cream of the timber claims in Oregon and Washington," Puter admitted to Heney, "were secured by Eastern lumbermen and capitalists, the majority of whom came from Wisconsin, Michigan and Minnesota, and nearly all of the claims . . . were fraudulently obtained."[19] Heney indicted thirty-four men, including Puter, Senator John Mitchell, former U.S. Attorney John Hall, U.S. Congressman John Williamson, Portland lawyer and state senator Franklin Pierce Mays, and state senator Robert Booth of Booth-Kelly Lumber Company. Puter turned over evidence to federal prosecutors that incriminated Senator Mitchell. Most damning was the $2,000 bribe Puter said he paid Mitchell. He had sought the senator's assistance, Puter testified before a grand jury, to convince federal land officials to approve the bogus land deals in Oregon. Mitchell was convicted of perjury and bribery.[20]

Mitchell's downfall had ramifications in Oregon politics. Joe Simon, a young railroad attorney who had been schooled by the senator and his law partner, Joseph Dolph, exploited Mitchell's disgrace. In his reforms and his career, however, Simon epitomized the political bossism and back room deals that characterized Portland politics at the turn of the century. Elected to the city council in 1877 at age twenty-two, Simon made no secret of placing the interests of his railroad clients, William Reid and Henry Villard, above those of the city. A year later, Simon was elected state central committee secretary for the Republican Party; in 1880 he was selected to be party chairman. From that post he secured a seat in the state senate, which he held for eleven years.

From 1880 to 1910, Simon was clearly a powerful individual in Portland and in Oregon State politics. By 1885, his forces controlled the city's district attorney and mayor, while Mitchell and his cronies held onto police, judge, and city attorney posts.[21] It can also be argued that Simon was the architect of Portland's political bureaucracy. Simon's greatest legacy was the Portland Board of Police Commissioners, which virtually ruled the city from 1885 until 1903. In a special legislative session in 1885, Simon convinced the Oregon State legislature to create a three-person police board that would exercise complete control over the police bureau. The board would eventually wield more power than any governmental body in Portland, holding the mayor and city council hostage. Oregon Governor Zenas Moody was authorized to name the first commissioners, with city voters electing succeeding commissioners. Governor Moody selected Byron Cardwell, a retired tax collector and Simon ally, appointed Simon crony Jonathan Bourne to the second chair, and rounded out the commission by appointing the board's creator, Joe Simon.[22]

Simon's rationale for creating the board was that it would control the police bureau, improve its efficiency, clean up the graft, and solve Portland's growing crime problem. Yet, by the century's end, the city property records listed thirty houses of prostitution and 110 saloons, with a growing transient population filling the city's hotels and boardinghouses. Entrepreneurs took advantage of the situation and organized the profitable vice enterprises of prostitution, gambling, and bootlegging. These activities often took place on land or property owned by the city's social, political, and business elite. Henry Corbett, John Mitchell, Henry Weinhard, and Joe Simon, as well as former and future mayors and judges were among the many businessmen who were linked to vice properties. City councilmen frequently represented the interests of the business community, which included the vice industry. These property owners ran the city and supported Simon's political machine. Despite the creation of the Simon-sponsored board of police commissioners, the city's vice operations remained untouched.[23]

Not everyone was happy with this state of affairs. Police Chief C. H. Hunt complained in 1891 that political pressure prevented him from enforcing anti-vice laws, and that a bribe to a police officer could overrule his order to close a gambling den or brothel. Speaking to the city council in November, Mayor William Mason, a turncoat from the Simon machine, proclaimed, "We lack the power to enforce the laws. . . . [We have] no control over the police force in our city. . . . Our police perambulate the streets day and night and we hear of no arrests for the violations" of gambling laws. Nor were citations issued for bars open illegally on Sundays. Mayor Mason argued that the anti-gambling ordinances were "a dead letter in our statute books" and asked the councilmen whether the police were the protectors of the people or "sharers of the spoils."[24] Mason went so far as to write a letter to President Benjamin Harrison accusing Joe Simon, then a candidate for an open seat on the U. S. Circuit Court of Appeals, of running the board of police commissioners as a political instrument. According to Mason, Simon bribed police officers and was responsible for the laxity of Portland law enforcement. The inability of Police Chief Hunt and Mayor Mason to enforce vice laws was directly related to the fact that the city's most influential men owned the vice properties.[25]

Frustrated by the inability, or refusal, of the police to enforce the vice laws, Hunt and Mason fully supported an investigation launched by the Portland Ministerial Association in late 1892. This group of civic-minded reformers and church ministers, similar to the Committee of Fourteen in New York City, proposed to investigate ways to control prostitution in the city.[26] However, the Ministerial Association became frustrated by the police board's unwillingness to cooperate with its investigation. Leading members of the city owned many of the seedy vice properties, and to the amazement of the local ministers who participated in the probe, fifty or more of these property owners were parishioners in their own churches. Cyrus Dolph, brother of Joe Simon's law partner Senator Joseph Dolph, and John Caples, Judge Julius Moreland's law partner, owned a building on the corner of Northeast Second Avenue and Everett Street that was known as a "hangout for prostitutes and thieves." Others who owned properties or were connected to vice operations in Portland included beer brewer Henry Weinhard, bank vice president William Smith, former Mayor Van DeLashmutt, water board member and president of the Northern Pacific Lumber Company Lauritz Therkelsen, and Joe Simon. The Ministerial Association named civic leader Henry Corbett as the owner of the city's largest wholesale liquor store—one that allegedly provided product to illegal drinking establishments. City leaders also had ties to illegal gambling. The three most notorious gambling dens in Portland at the end of the nineteenth century were the Brunswick on Southwest Third, owned by former Mayor David Thompson, the Arion on Southwest Yamhill, co-owned by Henry Corbett, and "a dive" on West Burnside and Second Avenue, owned by Portland Savings Bank.[27]

While not every member of Portland's establishment was involved in the city's lucrative vice industry, some nonetheless were ridiculed for not taking a stand against the Rose City's dirty little secret. Harvey Scott, powerful opinion-maker and editor of the *Oregonian*, was criticized for his lack of participation in efforts to clean up the city and failure to publicize the vice investigation. In response, Scott protested that those concerned with the maintenance of the abuses were "the principal men of the city," the men of wealth on whose patronage the paper relied. Scott could not afford to alienate the most important men in Portland.[28]

When a member of the city's elite was caught engaging in illegal activities, the establishment went into action. Take, for example, the case involving businessman and politician James Lotan. In the early 1890s, Joe Simon and other officials in the Republican machine appointed Lotan to various local and federal government positions as a reward for his important services and loyalty. After Joe Simon left the state senate in 1892, Lotan was handed the reins of the party leadership.[29] In early December 1893, however, Lotan was indicted in federal court for smuggling over four thousand pounds of opium into Portland while serving as a U.S. customs collector. Lotan was found to have directed the Portland end of a drug-smuggling ring worth hundreds of thousands of dollars. In his trial, Charles Fulton, a future U.S. senator, defended Lotan, while Simon and his associate John Gearin defended others involved in the smuggling operation. The federal judge in the case was Charles Bellinger, a former partner of Simon and Gearin, and the jury foreman was Charles Ladd, fellow Arlington Club member of Lotan, Bellinger, and Gearin, and business associate of Jonathan Bourne, Lotan's close friend. The jury convicted ten members of the drug ring, but deadlocked on Lotan. After Nat Blum, an important witness for the prosecution, disappeared, the government dropped plans for a retrial. Lotan, a member of Portland's upper class, survived the ordeal.[30]

The lords of late nineteenth-century Portland believed in "open vice, openly arrived at," and this attitude carried into the next century.[31] In 1898 Hayes Perkins, a credulous itinerant laborer and sailor in Portland, described "blocks on blocks given up to prostitution, gambling, saloons and every variety of dive the world holds. From

First [Street] to Seventh, from Glisan to Burnside, there is nothing else but the underworld." The local police, Hayes explained, turn a "blind eye . . . to vice and robbery of drunks. . . . Then there are the endless rows of girls who play tick-tack on windows as one passes by. Tired smiles radiate from painted faces as they beckon the unwary to visit their boudoirs."[32]

By the turn of the century, prostitution openly flourished, with the red-light district stretching thirteen blocks from Northwest Everett south to Salmon Street, about one block from the county courthouse and only two blocks north of city hall.[33] It is difficult to imagine this development without the support of people in power. In 1903 Fred Merrill, a representative of Portland's North End, an area within the red-light district, won a seat on the city council by running on a platform to "keep Portland wide open." A defender of prostitution and gambling, Merrill suggested that the city would benefit from licensing the industries and by having prostitutes, landlords, and gamblers pay their share of taxes. Merrill claimed he was anti-establishment; he voted against corporate interests and blocked city contracts that benefited the political machines. Meanwhile, Merrill's friend, the shrewd Judge Henry McGinn publicly and financially supported Portland's vice industry. Appearing before the board of police commissioners, Judge McGinn petitioned the panel to consider a vice policy that would not be a "detriment and injury to the business community." The judge persuaded Commissioners David Solis-Cohen, C. N. Rankin, and George Bates to adopt a more lenient stance on vice crime. Commissioner Solis-Cohen was a close friend of Joe Simon, who in turn was the brother of Judge McGinn's law partner. Commissioner Rankin worked for the *Oregonian*, which was edited by Judge McGinn's dear friend Harvey Scott. Meanwhile, Commissioner Bates rented property to gamblers.[34]

Portland's experience was not unique. In fact, Progressive-Era reformers argued that gambling, alcohol, and prostitution were growing problems in every city. The Progressive Era has been broadly defined as starting in the 1880s and lasting through the 1920s, and is characterized by the various reform movements that attacked government corruption, monopolies, and sanitation. By the turn of the century, reformers throughout the nation struggled with issues of morality and the popularity of local saloons, gambling parlors, and brothels challenged the popular Progressive movement. In the latter case, Progressives said innocent young women were attracted to cities in search of work and a new life, but they often suffered economic disappointment and were forced into brothels. In most American cities, these women were rural-to-urban migrants or immigrants, such as Russian, German, and Irish immigrants in New York and Asian immigrants in Portland.[35] There were fifty-six female "boardinghouses" in Portland's Chinatown in 1900 that contained both Chinese and white prostitutes.[36]

Progressive reformers—mostly of the affluent middle class—attacked Portland's vice operations; they supported reform-minded politicians, lobbied for anti-vice city ordinances, and organized vice commissions to publicize the problem and put pressure on city leaders to cleanse the city of the immorality. Oregon was a leading progressive state and Portland in particular sought to address the problem of moral and political corruption. As historian Robert Johnston suggests, "During [the Progressive Era] . . . the Rose City was one of the most fertile grounds for the construction of our national civic life, as ordinary citizens vigorously thought through how the United States might come to grips with social changes such as the rise of Big Business, the role of popular sovereignty as politics moved away from partisan spectacle, and the increasing ability of experts to define appropriate behavior for the masses."[37]

To improve living conditions and ensure urban residents personal security and order, many civic leaders sought more efficient governance to address disorder inherent in the explosive growth of cities. Democratic Mayor Harry Lane, who won a stunning upset victory in the mayoral campaign of 1905, launched one of the more celebrated attacks on Portland's entrenched establishment politics and the vice industry. Lane was Portland's first public officer who was later appropriately remembered as a "social hygienist."[38] He was practical and honest, and did not seek public office for personal financial or social gain.[39] Although Mayor Lane lived on the east side of the Willamette, he refused to let the river get between him and his city. In fact, Lane was the first Oregon-born mayor and the first mayor from the eastside, thus untainted by the system of graft and patronage practiced by Portland's establishment on the westside. Like his fellow reformist mayors in Cleveland and Detroit, Mayor Harry Lane attacked political fat cats at the polls. In the 1905 mayoral race, Lane defeated Mitchell Republican George Williams on a platform supporting the working class and as a progressive businessman opposed to corporate interests and political corruption. Characterized as a "graft hunter," Lane's administration is most remembered for its fight for morality and humanity.

As mayor from 1905 to 1909, Lane did not hesitate to accuse other city leaders of corruption and inefficiency. His biggest battles were fought in city council chambers, where the majority of the governing body represented the interests of Portland's business community, the railroad and liquor interests in particular. Thomas Devlin, Lane's opponent in the 1907 mayoral race, represented the liquor industry and campaigned on the slogan, "The reformer ultimately fails."[40] Devlin was correct. After his re-election, Mayor Lane recommended that the council revoke the licenses of establishments that were conducting illegal activities. When irregular vice raids proved ineffective, the frustrated mayor resorted to ordering the dismissal of every police detective in the bureau. Yet Lane's movement to "cleanse and uplift the evil city, and make it morally and physically safe for families, single working women, and children" commanded little support from the city council and the business community.[41]

The trial of restaurateur Thomas Richards illustrates what Lane was up against. Richards owned the aptly-named Richards' Place, a restaurant on Southwest Park and Alder streets that was a front for a brothel. The trial turned out to be a farce, as both the judge and county clerk had friends in the liquor, gambling, and prostitution business. Subpoenas were stolen and false ones issued, and in the end Richards was acquitted.[42] The trial, the *Oregon Journal* editorialized, teemed "with suggestions of the rankest jobbery."[43] The building's owner was North Pacific Lumber Company President Lauritz Therkelson, who happened to be one of the city's most prominent business leaders and a member of the water board. When Mayor Lane recommended revoking Richards's license, the city council declined to act.[44]

Mayor Lane's tenure in city hall ended after two terms in office. His four-year effort to reform city hall and destroy the vice industry showed meager results. Of the 169 ordinances the mayor vetoed while in office, including lucrative city contracts, nearly half were reversed by a business-friendly city council.[45] When Joe Simon and the Republicans won all of Portland's municipal offices in the 1909 election, including the mayor's office, it was clear that big business and political bossism ruled the city.

Joe Simon, Portland's mayor from 1909 to 1911, appointed many businessmen with ties to the liquor interests to executive positions. In fact, Simon made his corporate cronies rich with his support for municipal bonds for city improvement projects. For example, the mayor was criticized for a street-paving project in Portland Heights for which the city paid nothing, but the cost to property owners was $30,000. This and other projects benefited the "paving trust" and stuck homeowners with the bills.[46]

Mayor Simon offered similar protection to his friends in the vice industry. He eliminated the red-light district and lifted the restrictions to where vice activity could operate, thereby allowing the prostitution business to branch out and each entrepreneur to expand his individual niche in the industry. An investigation conducted in 1911 by the Portland Municipal Association, a group of civic-minded men and church ministers, cited ninety-eight known houses of prostitution that were doing a "booming business" in the

Rose City. The association blamed Mayor Simon for the city's vice problem, which they attributed to his appointment of A. M. Cox to head the police bureau. Cox had a reputation for being blind to vice and, on April 29, 1911, a Multnomah County grand jury indicted him for malfeasance in office, based on the suspicion that he had permitted gambling and prostitution to operate without interference. Shrugging off the allegations, Cox testified that Portland's vice situation was not his responsibility as the city's vice policy was determined higher up in city hall.[47]

The publicity surrounding the professional demise of the city's top policeman caught the eye of many Portlanders. Progressives were discouraged and frustrated that previous reform efforts had failed and by the fact that prostitutes, bootleggers, gamblers, and corrupt municipal leaders were harming the reputation of the Rose City. Within one month of A. G. Rushlight's election as mayor in 1911, another vice investigation was initiated, similar to the one launched in 1897. This time, however, city hall officially sanctioned the investigation. The mayor created a fifteen-member vice commission led by the upstanding Rev. Henry Talbot of St. David's Episcopal Church. The commission went block-by-block looking for evidence of immoral action. The first of their many reports was released in January 1912, claiming that the vice industry was rampant and lucrative—a fact that was no surprise to the city's residents. Talbot's group investigated 547 hotels, apartments, and rooming and boarding houses and found the majority, over 430 locations, to be "immoral."[48] In their final report, published in 1913, the commission determined that an initial investment of $1,000 to open a vice property made the proprietor $5,400 in the first year. Because fines for operating a vice property averaged $250, even enforcement did not deter operators.[49] As the *Oregonian* commented, "We can squarely face the fact that social vice is a large and powerful business and that it exists and spreads because it pays heavy profits."[50]

The vice commission drew a map of the city's vice houses in an effort to connect owners to their properties. However, the addresses were rendered indecipherable, apparently to protect the names and reputations of Portland's distinguished property owners. The commission even went so far as to destroy certain files in order to preclude the identification of those who owned the properties. Historian E. Kimbark MacColl diligently reconstructed the vice commission's map and determined "with a high degree of accuracy" the names of many of the property owners.[51] These included some of Portland's "best people."[52] A partial list of property owners and managers included the First National Bank, whose board members included Henry Corbett, Henry Reed, and Joseph Dolph. The U.S. National Bank, as well as Henry Weinhard and other powerful bank directors, also managed questionable properties. The rolls of Portland's major social clubs and civic organizations were also well represented on the vice commission's map. "The business-political leadership," MacColl later explained, "had closed its eyes to the problem, collected its profits, and prevented any effective reform."[53] In an attempt to exculpate himself, Joe Simon, ex-mayor, Republican boss, and chief representative of the city's political community for more than twenty-five years, apparently sold his vice-related property following the publicity surrounding previous anti-vice campaigns.[54]

From the state capital in Salem, Governor Oswald West pressured Mayor A. G. Rushlight to clean up Portland. "The real prostitutes . . . in Portland are the prostitutes in office," Governor West proclaimed in August 1912.[55] "There is a great deal of property held by people of means that is rented for houses of prostitution. . . . That property is held by corporations organized for the purpose of 'covering up' the real ownership."[56] For many upper-class citizens, historian MacColl found that prostitution was a "necessary evil" in Portland; it was "a process by which the young men of the family could achieve initiation into the mysteries of sex before entering upon marriage." Prostitution was socially acceptable, a "necessary amusement," and "for the unhappily married, an indispensable relief."[57] This was similar to New York City at this time, where brothels thrived in the entertainment districts scattered across the city and maintained symbiotic relationships with theaters and other establishments that either tolerated or openly encouraged prostitution.[58] Above all, prostitution in Portland was too profitable to destroy, especially for landlords and law enforcement officers who received a share of the money, and since the liquor and gambling industries were closely tied to the brothels, destroying these operations was also difficult.

In an attempt to clean up the Rose City, or at least to make property owners take responsibility for the crimes committed on the premises, the Portland City Council passed an ordinance in 1912 requiring owners of hotels, apartments, boarding houses, saloons, and other lodgings to post a sign, or "tin plate," designating the name and address of the owner or owners. This was clearly meant to shame the property owners into clearing out prostitutes. The ordinance, however, did not specify that the nameplates had to be in English; some were displayed in Hebrew, Arabic, and French. The ordinance was subsequently amended stipulating the signs had to be in English.[59]

While the vice commission's report of 1912 made city officials and voters aware of the prostitution problem, another damning report exposed the depths of Portland's corrupt political bureaucracy. In March 1913, progressive state officials solicited the New York Bureau of Municipal Research to investigate Portland's municipal operations. The New York bureau concluded that the police bureau was unorganized, inefficient, and the officers improperly trained.[60] Its report described Portland as a "sanctuary of rats, flies and mosquitoes. There is no fear of the plague. . . . Garbage collection is a disgrace to any city."[61] The report also concluded that many other city departments were equally mismanaged. For example, consumers were charged "more than twice what it costs to deliver water," and "Portland has no budget."[62]

The New York–based investigation prompted a rapid response from community leaders, and within a year, Portland voters approved the so-called Galveston Plan of government. In September 1900, a hurricane and the massive tidal wave it created destroyed most of Galveston, Texas. Later hailed as the "Storm of the Century," it leveled more than 3,600 buildings and killed six thousand of the city's residents.[63] After city officials failed to act quickly or sufficiently to help the refugees, political reformers in Galveston adopted a new city charter that replaced the mayor and city council with an elected nonpartisan city commission. Thus, a more professional model of urban management was adopted by many U.S. cities, including Portland in 1913. The Galveston Plan made each councilman responsible for an individual department to ensure accountability. As important, the new system was designed to prevent political bossism and corruption. The new form of government replaced Portland's fifteen part-time city councilmen with four, nonpartisan, full-time commissioners and a full-time mayor. Each commissioner and the mayor was assigned at least one city department with the mayor normally responsible for law enforcement. The commissioners and the mayor held equal votes in legislative and administrative decisions, thereby nullifying the possibility of an executive veto. The transition to a new system represented a victory for old and new progressives, liberal Republicans, planning advocates, environmentalists, and middle- and working-class citizens in Portland.[64]

In addition to this new system of municipal governance, the state legislature, moreover, enacted the Abatement Law of 1913, which specified that "anyone owning a building used for immoral purposes was guilty of maintaining a public nuisance."[65] The illegal activities did not have to be witnessed—"common fame" was sufficient to establish guilt—and investigators were not required to prove the owner had any knowledge of the vice operations.[66] The building would be padlocked, furnishings confiscated, and offenders could be fined and jailed. In August 1913, District Attorney Walter Evans filed the first of many suits under the new abatement law, which struck at many prominent family estates. Evans eagerly filed sixty-eight suits over an eighteen-month period, and over the next four years he attacked the city's vice industry. Evans was so enthusiastic about his vice crusade that in 1917 newly elected Mayor George Baker had to pull him in and calm him down, while withdrawing city support for the crackdown. The police bureau could not figure out what to do with all of the prostitutes. The election of Mayor Baker signaled the end of the short-lived vice crusade, as the nation had become involved in the Great War and city appropriations were now directed to the war effort.[67]

Anti-vice campaigns were not resurrected with the end of the war. Instead, 1919 saw the ratification of the Prohibition amendment, which exacerbated the problem of municipal corruption. The illegal distribution and sale of alcohol was the perfect breeding ground for law enforcement graft. In the fall of 1920, the *Oregon Journal* accused the Portland Police Bureau of conspiring with bootleggers. The newspaper further accused Mayor Baker of "mismanagement and ineffective enforcement" of existing vice laws.[68] According to Floyd R. Marsh, a police officer assigned to Portland's vice squad, city leaders were exempt from national prohibition. "I recall one instance that I was ordered to take some [confiscated] whiskey to a City Commissioner who had a summer home near Mt. Hood. I went to the Police Station and loaded my car with 11 quarts of bonded Scotch Whiskey and headed for Mt. Hood. Since I would be going the wrong way for an alibi [traveling from instead of to the police station with the alcohol], I kept my eyes peeled for Federal Agents."[69] What made it even more frustrating for Marsh was that while he was on the streets arresting and jailing people on alcohol-related charges, "the City Hall crowd and their friends" were drinking all the evidence.[70]

Because of its river ports and its close proximity to wooded areas, Portland quickly became a major distribution point for Canadian whiskey and local moonshine. Liquor from Canada was brought up the Columbia River and distributed at Sauvie Island to Portland speakeasies or given to runners who transported the bootleg to other towns. During the 1920s, a time when the manufacture and distribution of alcohol was outlawed, as many as one hundred speakeasies and one hundred beer and wine parlors were operating in Portland. "Most of the speakeasies paid police protection money totaling over $100,000 a month," Marsh explained.[71] A visitor to Portland suggested that prohibition was enforced so well in Portland that whiskey was priced $30 a case higher than in Seattle. "One might deduce from this remark," MacColl later commented, "that Portland's police were simply asking and getting a higher than normal price per bottle from their well stocked basement warehouse."[72]

One of the by-products of a productive bootlegging industry was a profitable gambling industry. Payoffs totaled about $60,000, with $20,000 going to police protection. Patrolmen normally received $10 per month directly, while city hall officials collected their payoffs from plain-clothes officers. Portland gambling dens were packed with patrons willing to take a chance during the fast-paced times, and young prostitutes had numerous opportunities to recruit clients.[73]

Such activities continued despite the failed efforts of Progressive-Era reformers—such as Mayors Harry Lane, William Mason, and A. G. Rushlight, and Rev. Henry Talbot's vice commission—to curb the influence of corrupt municipal officials to enforce laws against vice and to preclude secret deals that promoted the economic interests of powerful interest groups. Even after the end of Prohibition, the bootlegger remained a fixture in the vice and economic community. When the U.S. Congress repealed Prohibition in 1933, the state of Oregon created the Oregon Liquor Control Commission and instituted a monopoly on the sale of alcohol controlling prices, licenses, and distribution. Thus, the bootlegger remained in business, organized unlicensed drinking establishments, delivered illegally imported spirits, and bribed law enforcement officers for protection. For the next twenty years, vice operations in Portland remained fully entrenched and vice racketeers continued to organize until a small group dominated the industry.[74]

TWO

POST– WORLD WAR II PORTLAND

ON THE EVENING OF JANUARY 14, 1947, FRANK TATUM, CAP-
tain of the merchant ship *Edwin Abbey*, went ashore for a night of
drinking and gambling. Wearing a cameo ring and platinum watch,
and carrying almost $700 in cash, he entered the Cecil Club on
Southwest Sixth Avenue—a small, unlicensed bootlegging joint with
gambling in the back room and prostitutes for those willing to pay a
little extra. Although the Oregon Liquor Control Commission raided
the club many times, the vice squad stationed a short distance away at
police headquarters ignored it. The following morning, Tatum failed
to report to his ship before its scheduled departure. After a weeklong
search by the Maritime Commission and Portland police, the skip-
per was found dead, with a broken neck, at the bottom of a 50-foot
cliff on Santa Anita Terrace in northwest Portland. His murderers,
it turned out, were three Cecil Club employees, including the club's
manager, Patrick O'Day. The three thugs beat Tatum, took his money
and the watch, and then threw him off the cliff, not realizing that the
fall killed the captain. One report claimed that their employer, James
Elkins—dubbed Portland's "vice czar"—had turned the men in to
the police, hoping to distance himself from the murder.[1]

The Tatum murder is one of many examples revealing that reform efforts in Portland had failed. Instead, Portland's post–World War II city hall and police bureau machinations resembled those of previous administrations, such as James Chapman (1882–1885) and Joseph Simon (1909–1911). Many other American cities benefited from successful reformist mayors, such as Raymond Tucker in St. Louis, Bertha Landes in Seattle, Frank Zeidler in Milwaukee, David Lawrence in Pittsburgh, and "Little Flower" Fiorello LaGuardia in New York, whose leadership and experience lifted these cities.[2] Portland, however, did not experience successful long-term reforms. Rather, during the 1930s and 1940s, vice crime became exceptionally well-organized as Mayors Joseph Carson Jr. and Earl Riley tolerated and profited from the vice industry. Even the aggressive reform efforts of Mayor Dorothy McCullough Lee and Portland's City Club did not ultimately hinder a flourishing Portland underworld.

By the spring of 1930, approximately three million Americans were unemployed as a consequence of the Great Depression; by 1932, fifteen million were out of work. Because of its depressed timber market, Portland's slump preceded the national one.[3] There are reports, however, that Portland's vice industry grew during this otherwise bleak period, and while the city lost $375,000 annually in liquor license fees during Prohibition, law enforcement officials and city hall continued to collect fees from bootleggers, gamblers, and madams, illegally supplementing their Depression-Era incomes in exchange for lax law enforcement policies.[4] Some historians assert that municipal corruption declined in America's cities during the years 1934 to 1945. The repeal of Prohibition, economic scarcity during the Depression, the bureaucratization of welfare services instituted under the New Deal, and the mobilization of the nation's war economy reduced the dominance of political machines and municipal corruption.[5] This conclusion, however, overlooks quite a different reality. Portland's vice industry, in fact, became exceptionally well-organized and consolidated by dedicated criminal figures that were unchallenged or even aided by corrupt law enforcement officers and city officials during the 1930s.

During the administrations of Mayors Joseph Carson Jr. (1933–1941) and Earl Riley (1941–1948), important municipal officers were chosen by political patronage, lucrative city contracts were awarded to friends of the administration, and the vice industry remained untouched. Both Carson and Riley were mainly concerned that municipal finances should maintain the appearance of law and order. Carson's tenure in city hall was easily characterized as "business as usual." His corporate connections, especially in the private electric utilities, contributed to a city hall record of little reform in the area of politico-business relationships. For example, he advocated that local industries have priority to the power generated by the Bonneville Dam and authorized police violence against dock workers during the Longshoremen's Strike in 1934.[6] Earl Riley, more than Carson, chose government by crony. "Give the people—usually one's friends—what they want," historian E. Kimbark MacColl later wrote of Riley's 1940 campaign.[7]

Riley's opponent in 1940, attorney Frank Hilton, unsuccessfully challenged Riley's legitimacy by presenting evidence of cronyism and corruption in municipal government. According to Hilton, Riley, dating back to his tenure as Portland's commissioner of finance, was connected to the corporate interests of Portland Electric Power Company and Northwestern Electric Company, each of which had been investigated by the Federal Power Commission for questionable political activities. Hilton also accused Riley of issuing licenses to brothels during his tenure as commissioner of finance. According to the Hilton campaign, "Operators and occupants of the bawdy houses" in the north end of the city signed an official "Riley for Mayor" petition.[8] In 1932, Commissioner Riley and three other public officials were indicted for accepting bribes in exchange for voting in favor of relocating Portland's public market from Fifth Avenue to Front Street, a move that benefitted large property owners. Despite an investigation, an attempted recall, and grand jury proceedings, the market was moved. Although the indictments were ultimately dismissed, it was later revealed that the city paid $200,000 above the asking price for the Front Street site, demonstrating once again how city officials were often quite willing to put private and powerful business interests above those of ordinary Portland citizens.[9]

The Hilton campaign was quick to point out that Riley's campaign chairman in 1940 was A. G. Riddell, a representative of Standard Oil Company of California, a petroleum company that sold fuel to the city of Portland. Hilton also maintained that the owner of Meier & Frank Company, Aaron Frank, used the full power of this retail giant to curry favor with Riley. Frank allegedly sought assurances for future labor contracts, parking privileges, zoning codes, and city inspections.[10] Hilton further revealed that Riley's friend Phil Grossmayer of Travelers Insurance Company secured premiums for city automobiles that earned the insurance executive over a million dollars.[11] In fact, the city's insurance policy registers and city council minutes from the years 1938 to 1949 indicate that there was no competitive bidding on the city's lucrative insurance coverage, and that the largest contracts went to Grossmayer.[12] Although Hilton managed to force a runoff, it was Riley who emerged victorious in the final election and served as mayor for eight years, including the turbulent war years. "The choices that molded Portland's future" during Riley's tenure, historian Carl Abbott argues, "were made . . . by hastily assembled committees and corporate executives with limited citizen participation."[13]

The wartime economic boom brought unexpected social and political problems to Portland. During the war years, the city's busy shipyards—including Commercial Iron, Willamette Iron and Steel, and Henry Kaiser's construction empire—manufactured more than a thousand oceangoing vessels worth $2.4 billion in U.S. Maritime Commission contracts, and following the passage of the Lend Lease Act in 1941, Portland also became a key supplier of ships to the Soviet Union. As in sunbelt cities like San Diego, Mobile, and

Tampa, the new employment opportunities in Portland's shipbuilding industry emptied the rural counties of Oregon and Washington, and at the same time thousands of men and women migrated to the Pacific Northwest in response to "help wanted" ads posted in eleven states. The Kaiser shipyards alone employed nearly 92,000 workers during the war. Kaiser's recruiting success was part of what precipitated certain social problems in Portland in the years after the war.[14] In fact, Mayor Riley allowed Edgar Kaiser, son of the famous industrialist, to appoint influential members to Portland's Housing Authority, an example of how city hall was catering to business interests.[15]

By 1944, Portland's metropolitan population bulged to 660,583, increasing by 32 percent since 1940. This growth prompted the Bureau of the Census to classify the Portland-Vancouver vicinity as one of ten "Congested Production Areas"—a category assigned to cities when wartime mobilization stretched a city's resources, such as housing and transportation, "beyond their limits." Los Angeles, San Diego, the Puget Sound area, the San Francisco Bay area, and other cities were also identified as troubled cities.[16]

Perhaps the most disconcerting byproduct of Portland's explosive population growth and economic boom during World War II was an increase in crime. The number of homicides in Portland increased over 400 percent between 1940 and 1945, aggravated assault rose nearly 50 percent, and rape 700 percent.[17] Yet, most common citizen complaints were directed at Portland's organized vice industry—principally prostitution, gambling, and bootlegging. Historian Carl Abbott argues that the influx of young workers contributed significantly to the alarming rise in vice activities. The average age of the new shipyard workers was thirty, and half of them were single. Commanding an average wage twice that earned by local industrial laborers, the new shipyard workers had extra money, which was frequently squandered on liquor, gambling, and prostitutes.[18] The workers did not have to travel very far to satisfy their desire to gamble, for shipyard dormitories were often sites for card games and pool halls. The problem was so intractable in Vanport—a company town built by the Kaiser Corporation—that professional gambling outfits were shut down one day by local law enforcement only to resume full operation the next. Local racketeers operated lucrative bootlegging and gambling joints in Portland, such as the San Anita on Southwest Park Street and the Saratoga Club on Southwest Fourth Avenue. These clubs operated unmolested by law enforcement officers because the owners and managers paid scheduled kickbacks to key city hall officials.[19] By the end of the war, concern over police graft and municipal corruption reemerged.

Eager to dispel rumors of an alliance with the vice industry, in 1941 Mayor Riley launched an organized attack—or the pretense of one—on gambling dens, bootlegging joints, and brothels. In the first two years of his administration, the police bureau charged 991 adults with prostitution, which was 164 more than were arrested in the following five years combined. In 1942, the bureau charged 105 adults for liquor violations, but the average number of liquor violations during the next four years barely exceeded fifty. The same year, the police bureau charged 493 adults for gambling. But once the highly publicized reforms got the desired attention, Mayor Riley went back to allowing the vice industry to flourish. In 1943, the arrests dropped over 40 percent.[20]

"Like a classic political boss," historian Carl Abbott wrote, "Riley protected the diverse business interests and special privileges" enjoyed by big business, organized gambling, and prostitution.[21] In a candid letter to Ben Hazen, president of Benjamin Franklin Federal Savings and Loan, the mayor admitted that "there is, no doubt, some gambling going on in Portland. There always has been and, to be frank with you, there always will be." Mayor Riley further explained that while he was able to control prostitutes and gamblers during the war, he believed that the policing of morality was not the responsibility of the city government.[22] After the war Riley appointed David Simpson of Norris, Beggs, and Simpson, and other corporate directors to Portland's Postwar Development Committee, a body that "literally ran" the postwar city, especially the mayor's office. The firm of Norris, Beggs, and Simpson managed the infamous Richelieu Hotel, one of the most popular locations for prostitution in the entire city. Historian E. Kimbark MacColl describes Riley's time in city hall accurately as "corrupt, morally insensitive, and generally impotent," and that the business community was partly to blame.[23]

In many cities across the nation, voluntary organizations of unsatisfied citizens, such as neighborhood improvement associations, mutual aid societies, ministerial committees, and city clubs, came together as pressure groups to influence city government and advocate for social reform.[24] Amid the rumors of Mayor Riley's alliance with the vice industry, the City Club of Portland initiated its own investigation into the city's vice activities.

Progressive Era–reformers and civic-minded business leaders created the City Club in 1916 at the Hazelwood restaurant in downtown Portland. Reacting to the perceived need to improve the tenor of public life, the City Club embraced moderate political change and social improvement by government action and local volunteer efforts. The club's structure mirrored existing City Clubs firmly established in Chicago and New York. Accordingly, the founders created a board of governors and set up separate subcommittees to address the club's interests in city and state elections and legislation, public health, and law enforcement. In 1916, the City Club's immediate interests included railroad transportation and shipping, Oregon's state constitution, and juvenile delinquency. By 1931, the City Club's membership totaled 467. In the following two decades, the number would more than double.[25]

In early 1945, the City Club's Public Health Committee published "Portland Public Health Enemy Number One," a study of the efforts to control venereal disease in the area.[26] The previous year, U.S. Army and Navy authorities had considered placing Portland "out of bounds" to military personnel because of the high rate of recorded incidences of sexually transmitted diseases. The May

Act of 1941 gave the secretaries of war and navy power to take any measure necessary, such as creating prostitution-free zones, to protect military personnel from venereal disease.[27] It is unclear whether the military investigation inspired City Club leaders, but nonetheless, after releasing its report, the City Club acknowledged that an increase in Portland's population and the stationing of visiting troops were among the factors that contributed to the number of venereal disease cases. The City Club, however, stressed that an increase in population and a decrease in moral standards were only part of the problem. The inadequate patrolling of streets, taverns, and hotels by Portland's police officers contributed to more prostitution and thus was indirectly responsible for the wartime rise in venereal disease.[28]

While the City Club found many brothels still in operation in 1945, the apathetic Riley administration claimed to have no knowledge of organized prostitution in Portland and cited the American Social Hygiene Association's earlier report that had given Portland a clean bill of health. Mayor Riley's own records, however, include a police survey documenting that 1,640 women were charged with prostitution between 1941 and 1946.[29] City Club investigators claimed that the Hygiene Association's last inspection was preceded by an advance tip-off to city hall. In fact, in a report to Mayor Riley on January 9, 1942, officers Walter Padrick and F. G. Rehberg stated that after investigating a list of more than forty rooms and hotels—including the popular Zenith Rooms, Cecil Rooms, Richelieu Hotel, the Saranac, and the Savoy—they had found "some to be closed and some had not [sic] girls." All of the establishments, the officers emphasized, had received warning of possible raids, and, the report's note "none running" indicated that business had been suspended at the time of the raids.[30] Despite public pronouncements that the city was relatively free from organized vice, the City Club uncovered copious evidence to the contrary.[31]

The City Club report of 1945 criticized the Portland police and Mayor Riley for having failed to adequately control prostitution. Prostitution remained illegal under municipal statutes passed in 1871, the City Club argued, yet police and city hall apparently favored confining the brothels to one area—in a red-light district— and sought to regulate rather than repress such activity. City officials insisted that closing these properties only led to the spread of prostitution to other parts of the city, making it more difficult to eliminate.[32] Historian Elizabeth Alice Clement found this was the case in New York City. As a result of progressive reform agitation, red-light districts were shut down, therefore, brothel prostitution declined. Consequently, individual women in New York were able to set up their own operations, thus spreading prostitution into small working-class commercial and residential neighborhoods.[33] The City Club of Portland insisted that the mayor and police chief uphold existing anti-prostitution laws, intensify police activities in streets, taverns, and dancehalls, and assign plainclothes officers, preferably women, to cooperate with public health officers.[34]

Two years later, the City Club launched another investigation as a continuation of its public health report on Portland. City Club leaders announced that the purpose of their investigation was to determine whether Portland was an "open town" where gambling, bootlegging, and prostitution operated unhindered and even sanctioned by law enforcement officials.[35] Introduced with much fanfare by the City Club's Public Safety Committee in February 1948, the report, "Law Enforcement in Portland and Multnomah County," became the first report in club history to make newspaper headlines. It accused city leaders of allowing and even profiting from the city's lucrative vice rackets.

City Club officials insisted their inquiry was neither intended to launch a moral crusade, "nor to carry the responsibility of determining or promoting what it might consider to be a sound or wholesome public or police policy toward vice." Its purpose was simply to inform the honest citizens of Portland of the state of their city. The public safety committee explained that its original goal was to determine the methods used in vice operations, the owners of such enterprises, and any affiliation they may have with organized crime. Thus, its investigation made inquiries into police methods of supervision, organization, and policy with respect to vice crime and the potential involvement of law enforcement officials in illegal activity. The committee pursued in particular any evidence of police corruption in the form of protection payoffs.[36]

The ambitious City Club committee carried out a broad, full-field inquiry into vice crime and police graft. It examined newspaper crime reports, as well as efforts to control vice and published texts on vice crime and municipal corruption in other cities. Club investigators even contacted Oregon Governor Earl Snell, Mayor Riley, city commissioners, and Police Chief Lee Jenkins and allowed them to contribute to and comment on the investigation. The committee interviewed current and former nightclub owners, operators, and their patrons, as well as any witnesses having information about the location, ownership, and operation of vice establishments. It obtained copies of official criminal and legal records that had been assembled by the police department and acquired a copy of the Vollmer Report of 1947, a study of Portland's Police Bureau completed by retired police chief August Vollmer of Berkeley, California.[37]

Subject to heightened public pressure and a large number of citizen complaints, in 1947 the Portland City Council hired August Vollmer to investigate the police bureau's operations. Typical of such complaints was that of citizen Mrs. Eugene Kinnicutt, who alleged to city officials that the police officers who responded to her emergency call showed up at her home clearly intoxicated.[38] Adding to the letters of complaint that deluged city hall were those alleging that officers used threats to sell tickets to the Policemen's Ball, that they used unprofessional behavior at traffic signal stops, and that officers failed to administer care or displayed callous indifference to injured individuals at traffic accidents. There were also complaints about police corruption. The Portland Trade Union Bureau complained about "special police officers" who had solicited merchants to provide nighttime protection for their businesses, but who had then failed to render the services agreed to and paid for.[39]

The significance of the Vollmer Report was its surprising revelation that during the war years, major crime in Portland soared past that of other cities having similar populations. August Vollmer also disclosed that incidents of vice crime, crime against property, and juvenile crime were particularly high, and concluded that Portland's Police Bureau was unproductive, poorly organized, and inadequately supervised. Mayor Riley had admitted in 1945 that the bureau's mismanagement was attributed to the use of temporary appointees, which comprised 64 percent of the city's police force. The bureau also suffered from constant turnover; Riley further conceded that the 36 percent of the police force who were permanent appointees were mostly "people who, by virtue of age, physical condition, or other reasons, should be retired."[40]

August Vollmer also determined that the bureau was financially inefficient and that officers were underpaid, which he believed was a principal factor contributing to the problem of graft. While Vollmer recommended better record keeping in all police bureau departments, he did not, however, recommend any specific action to combat Portland's vice problems other than the confiscation of gambling machines and paraphernalia, believing these to be at the center of "rackets" all over the country.[41]

The Vollmer Report was instrumental in providing the City Club investigators with data on crime in Portland as well as on problems in the police bureau, such as corruption and mismanagement. Club investigators supplemented the specific examples cited in the Vollmer Report with information obtained from police bureau files. These files listed 248 known locations where gambling, bootlegging, prostitution, and other illegal operations took place; they also listed 185 addresses where arrests were made for gambling and prostitution. Combining information gathered at the county assessor's office with tips from former federal investigators, City Club researchers visited Portland-area nightclubs, gambling dens, and brothels and found that ex-convicts operated many of the establishments either themselves or through fronts. The club concluded that a definite group, which they referred to as a syndicate, controlled all organized gambling in Portland. An operator of a gambling den, for example, would lease slot machines, dice tables, and other casino paraphernalia from this group. Should the owner attempt to lease or buy equipment elsewhere, thereby disturbing the syndicate's monopoly, he usually found his establishment threatened or deliveries interrupted. According to the City Club, the syndicate received a percentage of the earnings from their gambling devices while protecting their clients from harassment by the police. Moreover, the City Club report noted sympathetically that local law enforcement officials claimed that they could not discriminate between the local bingo games held in churches and slot machines housed in gambling dens.[42]

Mayor Riley and Police Chief Jenkins made no apologies for the city's thriving vice industry, but insisted that Portland kept gambling, prostitution, and bootlegging to a minimum and that the number of vice establishments operating was normal for the size of the city. It seemed Portland's law enforcement leaders imposed an unofficial "tolerance policy" toward vice activities, similar to an official policy established by the city of Seattle. In that city, the tolerance policy allowed gambling establishments to operate as long as the maximum bet did not exceed one dollar, a clear violation of state law. The Seattle city ordinance gave law enforcement officers complete discretion to choose who could operate gambling dens. This discretion was based solely on a system of payoffs to police officers and their superiors.[43] According to Mayor Riley and Police Chief Jenkins, a policy of toleration and cooperation in Portland was easier to administer than trying to police the illegal activities all over the city.

Rejecting this explanation, the City Club accused the city police of protecting vice operations—particularly those aligned with certain crime syndicates. "This protection," the club asserted, "is provided in consideration of a substantial 'payoff' to some police officers and public officials." According to the City Club, such payments amounted to approximately $60,000 per month.[44] Vice establishments that kept up their payments to city hall and the police bureau were informed, or tipped-off, before a raid, thereby giving regular customers the chance to disappear before police officers arrived on the scene. E. Kimbark MacColl suggests that Mayor Riley himself personally skimmed off the lion's share of the $60,000 in monthly payments. The money was allegedly kept in a special vault installed in a room constructed adjacent to his city hall office.[45] A later investigation launched by the U.S. Senate Subcommittee on Investigations linked Mayor Riley to local gambling racketeer Al Winter, although it is possible a larger criminal syndicate was paying off the mayor.[46]

The publicity generated by the City Club report caused considerable anxiety at city hall. The day before the report was to be released to the public, Mayor Riley attacked the club's investigation as "politically motivated." The report's data, the mayor insisted, was misleading and did not prove the existence of any connection between city hall and the city's vice industry. Mayor Riley went so far as to claim that some members of the club's public safety committee had themselves sought city offices and municipal posts, and that they were issuing the report for "trading and political purposes."[47]

Yet not even Mayor Riley could ignore the hundreds of letters that had been written to him by Portlanders prior to the release of the City Club report. Although many of these letters cited the names and addresses of known vice joints, the mayor responded either by denying that any illicit business was being conducted on the properties or by claiming that the business conducted on the premises was legal. One such correspondent, Reverend Harry Holtze, had frequently provided the mayor with information on vice establishments operating not only within the city, but sometimes within sight of a police precinct. Refusing to admit that he supported the city's lucrative vice industry, the mayor both denied that this illicit business took place and requested that the reverend provide proof of illegal actions.[48] Mayor Riley's typical response to complaints was the following letter to H. R. Dinger, dated April 3, 1946: "I do not know the source of information you have . . . the place is not operating as a gambling joint."[49] Dinger proceeded to return the mayor's letter with a note signed by Amy Dinger, either Mr. Dinger's wife or daughter, scribbled on the bottom of the page: "Dear Mayor—Are you kidding? I was an innocent bystander there a short time ago as the guest of some friends."[50]

The City Club report concluded that Portland was an "open town" with a well-defined system of bribery. The club investigators charged that bootlegging, prostitution, and gambling had become so open that "no police officer or public official competent enough to do his job could be unaware of the situation."[51] The researchers cited ninety-five articles in the local press over a twelve-year period that reported on some aspect of this problem. "Public interest and apathy," the report noted, "follow a regular pattern, like the peaks and valleys on a seismograph."[52] Typically, initial publicity in the press would stimulate public awareness of criminal activity in the city and accordingly would produce a "violent" reaction in the police bureau; this would inevitably result in generating more publicity surrounding a rash of raids and arrests, such as those seen during the first two years of Mayor Riley's generally indifferent administration. When the publicity diminished the criminal underworld would settle back into its normal routine until public condemnation, political reaction, and law enforcement activities were initiated once again, whereby the pattern would repeat itself. In their defense, several police officers explained to City Club investigators that they had found it difficult to enforce laws "which they felt the general public was not interested in having enforced."[53] Many members of Portland's establishment belonged to clubs, such as the Elks, American Legion, and other organizations, that used gambling for both entertainment and as a source of revenue. Nevertheless, champions of morality, such as church leaders and civic organizations like the City Club, feared the city's image would be tarnished, that tourists and new businesses would not be attracted to the Rose City, and that this blatant public immorality would corrupt young Portlanders.

The City Club concluded that just as bootlegging and gambling rackets were uncomfortably close to officials in city hall, its investigators also found that prostitution was no longer restricted to a single red-light district, as had been previously reported by the Portland Vice Commission in 1912. Although the majority of the brothels were concentrated in specific areas, they were not confined to a single section of the city. Furthermore, brothels such as the Saranac and Atlas Rooms, both located north of Burnside along Northwest Sixth Avenue, and the popular Richelieu Hotel, between Burnside and Northwest Couch, continued to operate despite a police report written in 1942 stating that the brothels had been closed.[54] Portland's brothels typically operated adjacent to bootlegging and gambling establishments, making them places of "habitual rendezvous for a considerable assortment of safe burglars, stickup men, dope peddlers, and other underworld characters."[55] The City Club reported that prostitutes and pimps frequently searched for customers at bootlegging and gambling joints.

James Elkins was a central player in Portland's vice scene. In fact, the FBI would later call him the city's "vice czar."[56] By the end of the 1940s, Elkins owned more than a dozen bootlegging and gambling joints, and used hotels like the Park Avenue and the Broadmoor to run his prostitution ring with little harassment from the police.[57] "He ran the gambling joints; he ran houses of prostitution; he ran everything. He was what they call a muscleman in the city of Portland," slot machine and pinball operator Stan Terry later explained.[58] Nightclub operator Nate Zusman told U.S. Senate investigators in 1957 that "Mr. Elkins ran the town."[59] Likewise, Harry King (a.k.a. Harry Huerth)—an accomplished safecracker and Elkins's friend and former partner—insisted that the vice lord was "the boss" of Portland.[60] The consensus among Portland's criminal underground was that Elkins was in charge. Commenting on vice in 1956, a former Portland police officer acknowledged that "this was the first time that one subject had controlled vice to the extent that Elkins controlled it."[61]

Born in Texas in 1900, James Elkins spent most of his first thirty years in and out of jail for crimes such as manufacturing moonshine during Prohibition, shooting a security guard during a botched robbery in Arizona, possession of narcotics, and various minor gambling offenses. Elkins arrived in Portland at the end of the 1930s and immediately became involved in his brother's small prostitution ring where he began to make connections for his own future vice operations. At first, Fred Elkins ran the houses and gave the money to Jim, while Jim paid off the police in exchange for protection. Jim's reputation among underground figures eventually rubbed off onto the local beat cops. "Even at that early period," Harry King explained, "he had a lot of connections with the police department."[62]

King's memoir provides a first-hand account of Elkins's rise to dominance in Portland's vice rackets, and much of King's recollection is corroborated by FBI documents, local grand jury testimony, U.S. Senate investigators, and other first-hand accounts. Elkins helped King secure a job repairing slot machines owned by Ray Enloe (a.k.a. Emlou), a gambling racketeer who in turn used Elkins to distribute his gambling machines. One day, while King was working on a machine, the Elkins brothers walked in with shotguns and took Emlou's operation from him, forcing the aging racketeer into retirement. "He [Jim] just told the guys that from then on they were working for him."[63]

A heavy drug user, James Elkins put King to work robbing drug stores for narcotics, promising King a good salary as long as the young thief kept his new boss fully supplied with morphine. "I would go out and find a drug store, rob it, give him all the narcotics," wrote King. "The understanding was that I was to keep him in narcotics. So, sometimes I would have to work once a month and sometimes I would work once a week. It all depended upon the amount of narcotics I got out of a drug store."[64]

Although Elkins was a drug addict, the available evidence suggests that he did not sell drugs. Instead, he put his efforts into gambling and prostitution. Elkins not only took over Emlou's gambling operations, but also acquired his contacts in the police bureau, building up this relationship "until he [Elkins] had full control of the department."[65] Elkins also forged a strong relationship with federal officials. He was, according to former *Oregonian* reporter Wallace Turner, a "source to the agent of the Federal Bureau of Narcotics" in Portland.[66] An FBI informant as well, Elkins furnished these law enforcement agencies with information on individuals or groups attempting to move to Portland for the purpose of establishing criminal operations. Informing was one way Elkins protected his own operations.[67] During World War II, the Elkins brothers worked with local navy intelligence officials in Portland, where they informed on those members of the Japanese community who were believed to be assisting Japan, likely a way of gaining the confidence of federal officials.[68]

With the end of the war, it was back to business. "We had all the gambling joints, all the bootleg joints in the downtown area, and nobody could open any place without an OK from Jim," Harry King reminisced. "We could double park our car out in the middle of the street and let it sit there. The cops wouldn't dare touch it because we worked for Jim."[69] Nate Zusman, owner of Portland's popular Desert Room nightclub on Southwest Twelfth Avenue and Stark Street, later testified that the head of Portland's vice squad, Lt. Carl Crisp, was a "stooge for Mr. Jim Elkins."[70] The relationship did not escape the notice of other police officers. One even suggested to state law enforcement officials that Lt. Crisp was closer to the Portland crime boss than he was to his own chief.[71] Local journalist Phil Stanford later explained that Elkins "owned the police, and with Lt. Crisp as his personal bagman, he [Crisp] set up a payoff for himself as well."[72] According to Stanford, Elkins distributed generous sums to the police department, paying off "every beat bull up to the chief of police" who, according to King, had been personally appointed by the vice lord himself. "Nobody got a promotion around there without Jim's OK first," King insisted.[73] Elkins's influence permeated every level of city government. He even financed the elections of two city commissioners in the 1940s. One was future mayor, Fred Peterson. This shrewd purchase allowed Elkins to secure a small voice in the city council; it also assured him of advance warning of any proposed anti-vice legislation.[74]

To maintain his hold on Portland's teeming vice industry, Elkins succeeded not only in securing official protection, but he also developed a scam that ensured him a virtual monopoly on gambling. As first explained by the City Club investigators in 1948, time and again, a small, local operator or an out-of-town racketeer approached Elkins hoping to buy into his operations. Elkins sold the operator a small piece of the action under contract, and for a monthly fee, allowed him to begin business in a few locations using his own machines. "There were two distinct payoffs in Portland," a former city police officer later explained. "One payoff was collected by members of the Portland Police Department and the other was collected by James B. Elkins."[75] Elkins further promised to "fix it" with the police so that the operator could schedule regular payoffs and operate unmolested. The agreement held up for a few weeks, but then "the bulls [police] would come and tell him the town was too hot" and the operator had to shut down for a short period. A few weeks later, the police informed the operator that it was safe to reopen. The payoffs then continued, but another shutdown occurred a few days later. Once the operator recognized the pattern and realized that he had no chance of making his gambling operation work, he finally gave up. Then, because the operator no longer made the scheduled payoffs to Elkins and the police, as stipulated in the contract, Elkins regained the locations plus the machines the operator was using. Elkins employed the same scam with madams seeking to open their own brothels within his jurisdiction. In return for startup fees and regular payments, the vice lord allowed the houses to operate without harassment. If payments slipped or were skipped, Elkins requested a police raid on the property.[76]

Elkins frequently pressured his local competition to demonstrate that he was in charge. Stanley Terry, at one time one of Portland's biggest gambling machine operators, recalls that the Portland Police once raided a tavern he controlled on Northwest Second Avenue and Couch Street. Terry drove to the local precinct and demanded to know why his machines had been removed and why Elkins and others were not being harassed like he was. As he waited to submit his complaint, an officer handed Terry the telephone: "This is Jim Elkins. What the hell do you think you're doing? You come and see me if you want to run a slot machine—you come and see me first before you put any slot machines around." So Terry left the police precinct and headed to Elkins's office on Southwest Second Avenue and Clay Street. While discussing the situation with Elkins, Terry heard a gun being cocked behind his head. Somehow he managed to maintain his cool.[77]

When it came to protecting his turf, Elkins showed little hesitation to get rough. When neither his scam nor his threats discouraged a Minneapolis crime syndicate from operating in the "open town," Elkins simply set fire to the group's club. Because Elkins owned the building, he also profited from the insurance payout. The Minneapolis mobster called his boss and told him they did not have a chance in Portland—Elkins had the industry locked up. Elkins ran the city so well, King wrote in his memoir, that he allegedly had outside offers to extend this set-up to other cities.[78]

These accumulating revelations of organized crime—publicized by the City Club, the Vollmer Report, and newspaper articles on municipal graft—led many Portlanders to believe that city hall was rife with corruption. The business community, real estate investors and developers, and the general public blamed municipal leaders for slowed job growth after the postwar boom subsided and advocated for progressive change.[79] In many cities across the nation, including Phoenix and San Antonio, progressive reformers in the postwar years renewed the fight against cronyism, political machines, vice crime, and corruption in law enforcement.[80] In Portland, Captain Frank Tatum's grisly murder in January 1947 was the tipping point. The murder illustrated that petty vice activities like gambling and prostitution were indisputably linked to violent crime in the city, and it triggered public indignation and demands for more effective law enforcement and municipal leadership.

Over the next year, many reformers pleaded with a woman named Dorothy McCullough Lee to run for mayor and tackle the vice problem. A former state legislator and municipal judge who had once been the youngest female lawyer in the state, Lee was a popular city commissioner in the 1940s. Because of her education and political experience, she was probably more qualified and had more political experience than any mayoral candidate before her. Friends, neighbors, former legal clients, and civic clubs told her that it was her duty to run for mayor. The release of the Vollmer and City Club reports publicizing allegations of graft in the police bureau and city hall only increased the pressure on Lee to declare her candidacy. "Many people seemed not too concerned with petty irregularities," Lee's husband wrote in a biography of his wife, "but most people were curious, uneasy, or frightened at the persistent stories of a systemized payoff."[81] Only after a City Club investigator privately confronted Lee with information omitted from the 1948 report did Lee finally decide that she could no longer sit back and watch Mayor Riley and his administration carry on a lucrative and deeply corrupt relationship with Elkins and other vice racketeers.[82]

On March 12, 1948, Dorothy McCullough Lee announced her candidacy. Campaigning on a promise to "enforce the law," Lee was elected with little financial backing, but with considerable popular support. In the May primary, she received a 70 percent majority, enough to avert a run-off in November. Because the victory was so easy, Lee believed she had the public's firm support and this misinterpretation of popular support would have a negative impact on her re-election campaign four years later.[83] Mayor Lee immediately replaced Riley's police chief with Charles Pray, a retired supervisor of the Oregon State Police, and ordered the police bureau to close all after-hours clubs. The mayor explained that she "disliked occasional drives" against crime that characterized previous administrations and declared that she would "enforce the law evenly and continually."[84]

With a new administration in city hall and increased public awareness, many Portlanders believed the city's organized crime problem had been addressed and that vice properties would disappear, and some did. In the face of Mayor Lee's aggressive civic reform policies and encouraged by the possibility of uninhibited gambling in the Nevada desert, prominent local racketeer Al Winter closed his Portland operations and opened the Sahara Hotel and Casino in Las Vegas in cooperation with other organized crime figures. Other gamblers who similarly felt threatened by Lee's aggressive policies followed Winter to Nevada. Mayor Lee's crackdown, however, did not extend to areas outside the city, and like Mayor Lane's previous efforts, Lee's reforms had their limits. Many of the vice rackets simply moved out into the surrounding counties where the operations seemed secure. Mayor Lee lacked the critical support needed from law enforcement officers outside the city, particularly Multnomah County Sheriff Mike Elliot.

Elliot's campaign, it turns out, was financed by local gambling racketeers who wanted a sheriff that would protect gambling in the county while Mayor Lee would surely drive it out of the city. Elliot's love of publicity actually moved him to stage extraordinary raids on gambling joints and confiscate gambling machines, although he usually selected clubs and taverns not operated by his campaign supporters.[85] Portlanders eventually learned that Elliot lied on his resume about his tour of duty as a marine during World War II and about his college education. When the *Oregonian* exposed his misrepresentations, the new sheriff threatened to sue the newspaper for libel. Elliot's troubles with the *Oregonian* worsened considerably when a few months later, reporter Wallace Turner found Elliot vacationing in Lake Tahoe, Nevada, with his campaign manager and two prostitutes. Turner later reported that the trip was sponsored by Fred Elkins, who made the arrangements and paid the expenses.[86] Portland's former vice rackets had a friend in Sheriff Elliot and now operated unrestrained outside downtown.

Within the city, the vice industries faced an aggressive reformer in Mayor Lee. Although Lee was undoubtedly concerned about the city debt, traffic, a housing shortage, race relations, and efficient governance, her obsession was the fight against organized crime. In her radio addresses called "Report to the People," Mayor Lee cited commission reports, news stories, and magazine articles as evidence of the national, not just local, dimensions of organized crime and vice. Maintaining that criminal syndicates aimed to control local government, the mayor suggested that outsiders, from as far away as Chicago, were involved in the city's gambling rackets (though there is little evidence to confirm this).[87] Before her inauguration, Lee had discovered that despite having been outlawed by city ordinance, slot machines continued to raise funds for gambling establishments. In the past, the law against slots was only selectively enforced with punishments, confined to those who failed to pay for city hall's protection. On January 13, 1949, however, just days after her inauguration, Mayor Lee declared her war on gambling machines. "Slot machines and other highly lucrative and corrupting devices will be repressed. The law will be enforced against them and it will be enforced impartially, without discrimination and regardless of where the slot machines are located."[88] According to historian Paul Pitzer, Lee believed the "most effective attack on organized crime would be at its roots, with local gambling, which meant slot machines and punchboards."[89] In a related attack on Portland's brothels, Mayor Lee sent District Attorney John B. McCourt a report listing those establishments that the police bureau already recorded as allowing solicitation by prostitutes. In the report, the mayor personally pressured the district attorney to force those establishments to clean up their operations. Lee's promise of aggressive action was directed not only at the vice industry, but at those in city hall and the police bureau who profited from relationships with crime figures.[90]

Mayor Lee's anticrime crusade elicited numerous threatening telephone messages, letters, and packages (most colorful was a dead fish wired to an alarm clock) from slot machine operators, gamblers, and members of the business community who feared that enterprises they profited from would be suppressed. Organizations such as the Press Club, Eagles, American Legion, and the Multnomah Athletic Club, whose members typically came from the city's upper class, strenuously protested the mayor's slot machine proclamation because proceeds from such machines helped pay club expenses. The Press Club alone netted $50,000 from slots in 1948.[91] Gamblers vilified the mayor after she introduced and guided the passage of an ordinance in April 1951 outlawing gambling on "any game, athletic contest, race or sporting event."[92] Keenly aware that gambling was closely connected to alcohol, Mayor Lee hoped that by repressing gambling, her administration would also close down many drinking establishments. "If we didn't have all those amusement devices that are illegally played, you wouldn't have as many outlets. You wouldn't have as many taverns."[93]

Mayor Lee encountered protests everywhere she went because of her uncompromising stance. Letters to Portland's daily newspapers criticized her and she earned nicknames like "Mrs. Airwick," "Dottie Do-Good," and "No Sin Lee." As Lee's husband recalled, "The hit dog always howls."[94] When the mayor and her twelve-year-old son were asked to throw out the first pitch at a minor league baseball game in 1949, a chorus of boos overpowered the applause as they approached the edge of the grandstands. After finally acknowledging the intensity of the opposition and purchasing a gun for protection, the mayor and her husband sent their children to boarding schools elsewhere to protect them from threats.[95]

The vehement reaction of vice operators and members of the business community was proof that Mayor Lee was successful in disrupting a long tradition in Portland's city hall of tolerance for corruption; it also guaranteed that her reform efforts would be short lived and ineffective. Disillusionment with the mayor was so great that in September 1949, a small group of businessmen, led by Maxwell Donnolley, filed a recall petition with the city auditor. Although Mayor Lee survived this recall effort, her anti-crime crusade lost a great deal of public support. Moreover, the mayor and her police chief did not have the support of their police force. In fact, Police Chief Charles Pray resigned in May 1951 after complaining repeatedly that he was the only officer at police headquarters who did not know the locations of the gambling dens, bootlegging joints, and brothels, and that everyone kept him in the dark. Mayor Lee replaced Pray with police bureau insider Donald McNamara.[96]

City Commissioner Fred Peterson defeated Mayor Lee in her bid for re-election in 1952. Peterson won the election by a 6 percent margin, possibly because Lee paid little attention to the campaign and assumed Portlanders would acknowledge her efforts and support her reforms.[97] The main cause of her defeat, however, can be ascribed to Mayor Lee's attempts to enforce current vice laws and enact new gambling legislation that "went well beyond what most of the voters wanted." Her crusade did not change the social reality of the city and did not fully understand the connection between Portland's political and economic community. Lee did not realize most Portlanders did not support her attacks on public morality.[98] While her administration differed radically in character from those of Mayors Carson and Riley in its clear advocacy for clean government, Dorothy McCullough Lee's downfall was her naïve assumption that she could run the city without input of the business community.[99]

Commissioner Fred Peterson's election constituted a "firm rejection" of municipal reform by Portland voters and inaugurated a renaissance in the close relationship between city hall and Portland's criminal underworld.[100] The *Oregonian* reported in August 1953 that vice crime operated on an even grander scale and was more accessible than it had been the year before. The newspaper uncovered evidence similar to that published by the City Club in 1948, despite Mayor Lee's three years of reform. Brothels accommodated walk-ins, bootlegging joints brazenly poured illegal alcohol, and James Elkins continued to operate most of the vice establishments without any interference from local law enforcement. The *Oregonian* further claimed that taxi drivers received payoffs for bringing business to the brothels and drinking clubs. L. J. Lampert, manager of the Radio Cab Company, justified the actions of taxi drivers, accusing city officials of failing to control vice and criminal syndicates.[101]

Mayor Peterson emphatically denied the report that criminal syndicates operated in Portland and instead cited an additional report filed five months earlier by the American Social Hygiene Association that uncovered no evidence of serious vice conditions. It was later revealed, however, that the administration convinced local vice operators to close down while the Hygiene Association conducted its survey. Challenging the report's conclusions, independent cab drivers and another large taxi firm confirmed Lampert's allegations of city hall indifference. Seventeen cab drivers were arrested for prostitution after the newspaper's allegations were published and, during a 1956 grand jury investigation, cab drivers testified that Elkins had paid them to deliver customers to his prostitutes, who were set up in hotels throughout the city.[102]

A later *Oregon Journal* feature story told a similar tale, reporting that graft in the Portland Police Bureau was as common in the mid-1950s as it had been during the time of the City Club investigation nearly a decade earlier. According to the *Oregon Journal*, in one incident a sergeant from Portland's East Precinct approached patrolman Jack Olsen and told him of a way to earn extra money on the side. The sergeant described a "little deal" employed at a Chinese restaurant on North Williams Avenue and Russell Street. In return for overlooking this operation, Olsen would receive $50 a month—what the article described as "smile money." The patrolman, however, was obligated not to tell anyone about the payoff, including his wife. After Olsen told his partner that he was not interested in the money and that the offer should be reported to the chief of police or the mayor, his partner allegedly explained, "Who do you think's running this thing?" Olsen reconsidered and decided to accept the payoffs, but he recorded the serial numbers of all the bills he received and marked them "J. O." He then took the money and the story to James Miller, chief crime reporter at the *Oregonian*.[103]

A few weeks after being tipped off by Olsen, James Miller was approached by Captain Robert Mariels to join the International Footprinters Association, a fraternal order for policemen and civilian associates. Miller hesitated at first, but was assured that the captain could find a sponsor to fund his membership fees. Curious about whom the sponsor would be, the reporter agreed to meet his unknown benefactor at a downtown restaurant, where he found none other than crime boss James Elkins.[104] After the two talked for some time, the racketeer shoved a "large wad" of money toward the reporter, in exchange for quashing the exposé. Elkins admitted to Miller that he controlled the vice crime syndicate in Portland, but when Miller explained that his editor at the *Oregonian* might ask him to write a story about the syndicate, Elkins tersely replied that it would be a "very poor idea." Miller refused the money, which made Elkins irritated and even rhetorically violent. His mention of how "people [were] being dumped in the Willamette River" was clearly meant to be a warning to the reporter.[105]

Though vice was prevalent in Portland during the early decades of the twentieth century, it was not until the post–World War II period that crime was as thoroughly organized and consolidated as it was in other cities like Detroit, New York City, Philadelphia, and Chicago. This emergence of organized crime was arguably a byproduct of the social instability and unprecedented urban growth that was managed by a corrupt municipal administration. During this period, James Elkins, like crime bosses in other cities, succeeded in cornering the market through violent threats, scams, and political manipulation. Elkins, however, did not originate the practice of paying off municipal officials—Portland already had a long tradition of municipal graft. A good businessman, Elkins survived Mayor Lee's reform movement and protected his vice operations from smaller criminal organizations. "They all underestimated Jim," "Box Man" Harry King remembered.[106]

Despite the efforts of reform groups, such as the City Club, or newspaper exposés, Elkins and other vice racketeers were generally successful because most Portlanders simply did not care. In the 1950s, Portlanders were like other Americans—mobile—and similar to an earlier turn-of-the-century phenomenon, they abandoned the city for the suburbs. Portland's upper- and middle-class citizens eventually recognized that the city was the center of all their problems—crime, taxes, and minorities—and they left.[107] The businessman who commuted to downtown each day, generally unconcerned about society's greater social problems, was unfortunately operating under the same misconceptions as his predecessors.

THREE

ELKINS VS.
THE TEAMSTERS

"WE SHOULD GET RID OF THE CHARACTER," MULTNOMAH
County District Attorney William Langley told Seattle mob boss
Joseph McLaughlin and Teamsters union organizer Thomas Maloney. Langley wanted vice racketeer James Elkins eliminated, not
because Elkins was the biggest crime boss in the Rose City and a
menace to society, but because he had double-crossed the crooked
district attorney. It is unclear, however, whether Langley wanted
simply to run Elkins out of town or to have him killed. "He's
cheated me and he's horsing you guys around," Langley complained
in 1955 to McLaughlin and Maloney. "You got too much, you got
too damned much patience with him. . . . He's a no-good bastard.
He won't treat anybody right. Except a bunch of dizzy policemen,
I guess. . . . He's doin' to you just like he did to me. He lied to me
once a month for four years."[1]

William Langley was elected Multnomah County district attorney in 1954 with the help of labor racketeers and organized crime
figures. Despite Mayor Dorothy McCullough Lee's efforts to crack
down on the city's vice industry from 1948 to 1952, law enforcement
officials, and her successor in city hall, tolerated, sanctioned, and

profited from the city's barely concealed vice economy. Progressive reforms of previous decades had clearly failed. Crime boss James Elkins and other vice operators continued their lucrative criminal operations with the cooperation of local policemen and a corrupt district attorney. By the early 1950s, word of Portland's reputation as a "wide open" city traveled north to Seattle, where racketeers, aided by corrupt Teamsters union officials, had been exploiting that city's criminal operations for years. Sensing an opportunity to extend their control to the vice industry in Portland, the Teamsters sought the help of local crime boss James Elkins, known to be the city's "vice czar." With Portland's mayor and the police bureau securely in his pocket, Elkins was in full control of the city's lucrative vice rackets.

In 1956, however, the existence of organized crime in Portland— especially Elkins's operations—was given wide exposure by *Oregonian* investigative reporters Wallace Turner and William Lambert. Using information provided by Elkins and other sources, the reporters uncovered the Seattle Teamsters' and racketeers' scheme to take over Portland's vice operations. Elkins later claimed that he had been reluctant to help the Seattle group insisting that he had been a pawn in the Teamsters' plan to penetrate city and state politics while seizing control of Portland's profitable liquor, gambling, and prostitution industries.[2] But most likely Elkins was attempting to con the group much as he had in previous scams to keep outsiders from infiltrating his turf. In the past, he had leased a few select vice properties to outsiders, collected a portion of the profits along with the lease payments, waited for the location to become established and lucrative, and then had the operation closed down by his friends in law enforcement. When this plan backfired with the Seattle racketeers in 1956, however, Elkins found it necessary to end his arrangement with the group before they double-crossed or killed him.

Appalling reports of Teamsters-inspired corruption from Portland, Detroit, New York, Seattle, and other cities induced politicians in Washington, D.C., to investigate union racketeering and to expose those labor leaders who, for their personal benefit, made a practice of exploiting honest, dues-paying union members. The negative publicity that resulted from the investigation had long-term consequences for the legitimacy of the Teamsters union. In fact, union officials spent the next three decades trying to clean up the image of their organization.[3]

Labor unions were founded in the spirit of Progressive-Era reform. Progressives were the first political reformers of the industrial age to identify corruption and mature capitalism as the primary causes of inequalities in power and income that plagued late nineteenth-century American society. During the Progressive Era, unionism became a mass movement. Between 1897 and 1903, the American Federation of Labor grew from four hundred thousand to nearly three million members. In an age of burgeoning nationalism, however, labor challenged basic American traditions. For example, socialists and communists marching for workers' rights threatened the nation's economic and political system, and this made many Americans uncomfortable.[4]

Nevertheless, labor unions were reacting to the growth of Big Business and emerged as a countervailing force determined to protect workers' rights. By the late 1880s, union members fought for shorter workdays and workweeks, higher wages, and better working conditions, especially for women and children. Like other progressive reformers, labor unions and their supporters advocated rapid and radical change in the way owners and managers treated employees. But, while the idea of protecting laborers was ultimately successful, some unions failed to maintain their progressive ideals. Some unions, especially the International Brotherhood of Teamsters, were eventually controlled by opportunists who embezzled pension funds and used the union in a way similar to organized crime syndicates. By the 1950s, the Teamsters union was in dire need of reform.

The International Brotherhood of Teamsters was founded in 1903 by honest, hardworking cart and wagon drivers who organized to bargain collectively for their common interests, such as overtime pay, shorter workweeks, and fairer contracts. When the Teamsters began to recruit unskilled laborers (generally, laborers who were hired for tough, physical jobs) in the early 1930s, the union broke from its traditional policy of limiting its representation only to haulers and delivery truck drivers. Some labor historians argue that this allowed the Teamsters to be more inclusive, more democratic. Nevertheless, the organization fragmented, with the result that Teamsters officials who had fought for collective bargaining, better wages, and safer working conditions were pitted against a new legion of tough organizers, some who were motivated to join the labor movement principally to acquire personal wealth.[5] By the Depression Era, the Teamsters were less a national union than a cooperative of haphazard labor locals with almost total independence.[6] The decentralization of the union, therefore, gave some leaders the freedom to use pension funds for personal loans and make questionable concessions to business owners in return for money and gifts.[7]

Politicians and anti-union activists highlighted the threat posed by corruption and criminal activity in the Teamsters union. Given the union's ability to control important industries, it could cripple the economy of cities and possibly the nation by disrupting regular business activities. Journalist Steven Brill explains that the Teamsters had the power to "paralyze apparently unrelated industries" and gain control of many U.S. industries simply by refusing to deliver merchandise, parts, or other manufactured and natural goods.[8]

By the 1940s, the Teamsters had become top-heavy with officials, and "internal oligarchies" exercised control over certain industries. After World War II, a large group of full-time labor officials, such as Dave Beck and Jimmy Hoffa, assumed the leadership of the union, thereby "open[ing] the door," historian Nelson Lichtenstein asserts, "to a whole set of corruptions that became an integral part of the postwar union mythos."[9] Corrupt behavior was almost an inevitable by-product of the new responsibilities that fell to union officials. Teamsters union officials negotiated and administered pension benefits, seniority systems, wage schedules, and unemployment and health insurance. They also directly lobbied local, state, and national legislators, endorsed candidates, and provided union members and money for campaigns. In several U.S. cities—including Portland—zealous union officials supported illegal and sometimes violent methods to gain control of lucrative industries from business leaders and to command political cooperation from local government officials.

Teamsters' officials first attempted to organize Portland's laborers in 1903 and had achieved some success, but local membership in the union did not develop significantly until the 1930s. The International Brotherhood of Teamsters and the union's president, Daniel J. Tobin, had refused to give any support to the Portland Teamsters because the small specialized locals that operated in the city, such as the General Truckers' Local 162, were weak in comparison to locals in larger West Coast cities such as San Francisco, Los Angeles, and Seattle, and were usually not permanent. All that changed, however, when Dave Beck rose through the ranks of Seattle's Teamsters Local 174 to take a position of power within the union, which would affect the prospects of the Portland Teamsters.[10]

Biographer John McCallum described Dave Beck in 1978 as quiet and cordial, but quick to flash a full-toothed smile, which brightened his bland, lobster-pink face. He did not drink or smoke, and exhibited the aura of a "super Rotarian booster right out of [Sinclair Lewis's] *Main Street*."[11] Beck's union career began before World War I when he became a member of the Laundry and Dye Works Drivers Union in Seattle. His was the only local to vote against a laundry drivers' strike in 1917. In the late 1970s, Beck told McCallum, "I still hate strikes," but admitted that strikes were necessary to drive union interests and force concessions.[12] After World War I, Beck returned to Seattle and went back to work as a laundry truck driver. As an officer for his local, he was allowed to join Seattle's Joint Council of Unions and, by 1925, he was elected secretary-treasurer. He worked his way up through the ranks of Seattle's local leadership, and eventually Teamsters union President Daniel J. Tobin hired him to be a general organizer for the Pacific Northwest and British Columbia. In 1937, Tobin appointed Beck chief organizer for the West Coast and, shortly thereafter, Beck convinced Tobin to create the Western Conference of Teamsters in order to control the various independent and precarious locals in the region. As president of the Western Conference, Beck organized and dominated the locals of eleven western states using Seattle as his headquarters.[13]

Under Beck's assertive leadership, the Joint Council of Teamsters organized a number of cities—including Vancouver, B.C., Los Angeles, and Portland—by using its manpower, money, and strike assistance to full effect. Once the Oregon Teamsters began to make progress, meetings were held between Seattle's and Portland's Joint Councils, thus establishing a high level of cooperation between the Teamsters' organizations in the two states. Beck's influence within the union grew commensurately.[14] Beginning in the 1940s, Beck managed to establish a solid base from which to operate and secured a position that gave some Seattle Teamsters officials the confidence to influence other unions and unorganized labor. Teamsters' leaders also strengthened their conviction that they could organize illegal industries. While federal officials suspected that Beck, who was elected president of the International Brotherhood of Teamsters in 1952, was directly involved in Seattle's vice industry, they were never able to confirm these suspicions and he was never prosecuted for any vice crimes.

But there is no question that Frank Brewster, Beck's number-one man in Seattle, was directly involved in vice activity and that he associated with organized crime figures. Brewster was born in Seattle and joined the Teamsters while driving a dray in 1913, at the age of sixteen, a few years before Beck joined as a laundry-wagon driver.[15] After serving in World War I, Brewster returned to Seattle and quickly worked his way up through leadership posts of Local 174.[16] Later, Brewster would play a critical role in Beck's quest for power and in the success of the Western Conference of Teamsters. In the early days, however, Brewster and Beck were both partners and rivals. The two men were "driving, tough, ambitious opportunists of the union rackets which opened rich opportunities . . . for men not handcuffed by fastidious ethics," according to anti-union journalist Westbrook Pegler.[17] Although they had a rocky relationship over the decades, Brewster supported Beck in the 1920s as Beck moved up the ranks in the union's leadership. In 1929, Brewster became secretary-treasurer of Seattle's Local 174 and was part of Beck's reorganization in Portland and Seattle in the 1930s. By 1953, Frank Brewster had reached the pinnacle of his career when he was elected vice president of the International Brotherhood of Teamsters and president of the Western Conference of Teamsters. At the time, many Teamsters and government investigators considered him to be second in the union only to Dave Beck, despite Jimmy Hoffa's growing popularity.[18] As a business agent for the Teamsters, Brewster reportedly headed the Teamsters' "goon squad," a term the FBI frequently used to describe those union members responsible for physical intimidation. To ensure that acts of violence and any resultant controversy would not tarnish President Dave Beck, Brewster, the FBI concluded, directed the union's strong-arm operations.[19]

In addition to his official duties as a Teamsters official, Brewster also had interests in criminal activities outside the union. According to FBI officials in Seattle, Brewster was "in control" of a Seattle "crime syndicate" that influenced Seattle's politicians and participated in the city's vice operations.[20] Other state and federal investigators concurred and concluded that Brewster developed a business and personal relationship with Seattle and Spokane vice racketeer Thomas Maloney. The basis of this relationship, investigators believed, was built on real estate and organized crime.

Among the most damning evidence the FBI uncovered was that Thomas Maloney, an established gambler, prostitute broker, and associate of Seattle's infamous Colacurcio crime family, was on the Teamsters union payroll as an organizer.[21] Brewster also reportedly arranged for Maloney to receive a loan from Local 690 to bail out his restaurant and gambling operation in Spokane.[22] Brewster's personal secretary later said that she frequently made travel arrangements for Maloney, which were paid for by the Western Conference of Teamsters. In August 1955, Maloney listed Oregon Teamsters leaders Clyde Crosby and Lloyd Hildreth as references for an apartment rental and informed the property managers that he was a business agent for the Teamsters.[23] Nevertheless, Maloney was a "first-class bungler" according to James Elkins. Brewster even reportedly said that "Tom Maloney is a blubberhead, blabbermouthed so-and-so, and I have known him for 20 years, and I have put him in business 20 times and he messes up every time."[24]

The FBI and the Oregon State Police also investigated Joseph McLaughlin, a.k.a. Joe McKinley, a Seattle crime figure and a close friend of Brewster.[25] Brewster once told Elkins that "Joe McLaughlin would be an asset to any man's organization."[26] The FBI insisted that McLaughlin was the leader of Washington State's McKinley mob, infamous in Seattle crime circles, and shared the city's vice rackets with crime boss Frank Colacurcio.[27] Federal investigators believed that Maloney and McLaughlin were part of Brewster's "goon squad" that had helped organize the beer, bakery, and pinball industries in Portland during the 1930s and '40s.[28]

By the 1950s, Frank Brewster and the Seattle racketeers were profiting from their city's vice industry. Once they heard from their contacts in organized crime that Portland's booming vice industry was ripe for organization, Brewster and his associates quickly recognized who they needed to approach for help. James Elkins, the brains behind Portland's criminal rackets, was their man. When Elkins wanted to place his gambling machines in the Portland Labor Temple in 1953, he visited Teamsters officials in Seattle. Soon enough an arrangement was made whereby Brewster and Teamsters Secretary-Treasurer John Sweeney gave Elkins permission to put his gambling machines in the Labor Temple in exchange for helping Thomas Maloney set up a small gambling operation in Portland.[29] As gambling machine distributor Stanley Terry later explained, John Sweeney was "kind of in bed with Jim Elkins."[30] Elkins, Brewster, and the Seattle racketeers ultimately agreed to organize Portland's pinball, slot machine, and punchboard operations—the same gambling vices that the union controlled in Seattle and that Portland Mayor Dorothy McCullough Lee and the city council had outlawed in 1949.[31] Punchboards, associated with gambling since the nineteenth century, were pieces of cardboard that had hundreds of small holes covered with paper. A gambler would pay the establishment's operator—the "bet" was usually a nickel—for the chance to use a metal pin to "punch" a hole and pull out a slip of paper that listed a prize of merchandise or cash. Pinball was sometimes unfairly associated with gambling machines because it was coin operated and was legally defined as a game of "chance," although by the 1930s some pinball manufacturers were building machines that paid out in cash, which was illegal.

Paradoxically, Mayor Lee's enthusiastic reform campaign of the late 1940s, which attacked gambling operations, set the Teamsters up to aggressively organize the pinball dealers association in Portland.[32] From the perspective of the gluttonous Teamsters officials, the prohibition of the gambling machines in 1949 presented an opportunity to bring the Coin Machine Men of Oregon, a union of gambling and vending machine distributors, into the International Brotherhood of Teamsters. While the Teamsters could control the distribution of gambling machines by dominating the trucking industry, vice racketeers Maloney, McLaughlin, and Elkins could use the Teamsters dominance to profit from a gambling monopoly. The effort to step in and establish control of the gambling machine industry paid off. By 1954, the coin-machine industry was organized, and local Teamsters official Clyde Crosby was ready to lobby the Portland city council to reevaluate the ordinance and legalize gambling machines.

The Teamsters' lobby effort was expensive. An Oregon State Police informant told investigators that the Coin Machine Men of Oregon collected "several thousands of dollars, somewhere between $5,000 and $10,000 . . . to be paid over to the City Commissioners in return for their voting in favor of allowing" pinball and other gambling machines to operate. The Teamsters' primary target was Commissioner Stanley Earl, who, before winning election to the city council in 1953, had been an officer for the CIO and the Industrial Wood Workers Union.[33] A federal labor advisor during the Korean War, Earl also worked as a bouncer for Fred Elkins, brother of James. Ironically, in 1948, Earl was the main City Club investigator and contributed to its report on the city's vice activities.[34] Although he had originally favored legalizing the pinball machines, Earl later testified that Clyde Crosby approached him on May 18, 1955, and told him that if he "did not support pinball legislation, licensing those devices, I would have the opposition of the Teamsters in the election in 1956." In the end, Earl voted to continue the ban, later claiming that he had changed his mind after learning from the wife of a railroad worker that her husband had gambled away his paycheck on pinball machines.[35]

As a consequence of voting against legalizing pinball machines, Earl lost the Teamsters' support in the upcoming election for city council. On February 23, 1956, the *Oregon Journal* newspaper reported that Teamsters union leader Clyde Crosby had been named chairman of the committee to elect Jack O'Donnell to replace Commissioner Earl. The announcement, the newspaper highlighted, was made independently of the endorsements being considered by other organized labor unions in Portland.[36] According to documents and receipts filed with the Portland city auditor, the Joint Council of Teamsters paid $4,874 for O'Donnell's failed attempt to unseat Earl.[37] Consequently, the ban on pinball machines was sustained.

Despite their failed attempt to legalize the gambling machines, the Teamsters could be satisfied that they had at least successfully organized the industry's distribution networks. The Seattle group's next plan was to monopolize the city's lucrative punchboard industry. Elkins, who controlled Portland's gambling machine industry, later told investigators that he had introduced Maloney and McLaughlin to Norman Nemer, a Portland punchboard distributor, in the hope of bringing Nemer into the union and making him their front. Recalling that at the time he fully understood that McLaughlin and Maloney were representing the Teamsters union, Nemer later explained that the union ordered him to hire Maloney as an assistant bookkeeper. Nemer was to receive union stickers to put on his punchboards, thereby distinguishing them from nonunion punchboards; businesses that used nonunion punchboards would face the Teamsters' pickets and would have their merchandise deliveries disrupted. In this way, businesses would be forced to use Nemer's equipment. In return, Elkins and Nemer would each receive 25 percent of Nemer's profits, and McLaughlin, Maloney, and the Teamsters would share the other 50 percent. The profits from this operation in Portland alone, Elkins later reported, amounted to approximately $100,000 a year. The plan began to fall apart, however, when Nemer became uneasy about McLaughlin's connections to Brewster, Sweeney, and Crosby, and when Sweeney complained that McLaughlin and Maloney would not get enough money. In the end, the plan was dropped.[38]

The Coin Machine Men of Oregon, a group controlled by Elkins, McLaughlin, and Maloney, used the same tactics to take control of the pinball industry in Portland. This time the front was Budge Wright, a Portland-based coin-machine distributor and the chief rival of Stanley Terry, a successful gambling-machine distributor (he operated outside Portland's city limits), whose union card had been withdrawn by the Teamsters in 1954. According to industry standards and especially the Teamsters, Terry was required to be a member of the union if he wanted to transport his machines by truck. Wright later recalled that McLaughlin had convinced him that his pinball operations would be backed by the economic and political power of the Teamsters union: "[McLaughlin] told me that talking to him was just like talking to Crosby and Sweeney."[39] Wright created Acme Amusement Company with McLaughlin and Fred Elkins and prepared to move in on the city's other pinball machine operations. Whenever Acme Amusement met opposition from business owners, Teamsters picket lines formed.

Among the Acme Amusement Company's first targets was the Mount Hood Café, where Stan Terry maintained his pinball machines. One morning in 1955, Portland Teamster Frank Malloy warned Horace Crouch, the owner of the café, that if he did not replace Terry's machines with Acme's machines, the Teamsters would picket the establishment. Crouch was a union member and was surprised by the threat. The pickets were not personal, Malloy told Crouch: "You take Stan Terry's machines out, and we will pull the pickets."[40] Crouch later lamented:

> I couldn't get coffee; I couldn't get bread; I couldn't get meat deliveries. I called these outfits up. I have been in Portland 30 years or more in business. They said, "Well, you meet me up the street and we will transfer the food into your car and you can haul it yourself." . . . Frank Malloy and another fellow followed me in the car, and got out and told the coffee man to take the coffee out of my car and put it back in his truck. I pulled out a monkey wrench, and I said, "Nobody touches this coffee. The first one that does will get this over his head. You better get in that car," I said, "and drive away or this wrench will go through your windshield." He got in and drove off.[41]

The Teamsters and Elkins applied the same pressure to business owners throughout Portland. Teamsters union President Dave Beck denied any knowledge of the group's activities, but the Teamsters moved to organize the coin-machine industry in other cities in much the same way as they did in Portland. Reportedly working in conjunction with organized crime figures, the union organized the coin-machine industry in Chicago, Cleveland, San Francisco, New York, and Detroit, among other cities.[42]

Beck's practice of creating "goon squads" laid the groundwork for a pattern of intimidation and violence that had characterized the union's earlier organizing methods. Beck also tolerated corrupt union representatives' use of the organization's resources, including participation in illegal activities. Teamsters' representatives in Portland disrupted businesses whenever Maloney, McLaughlin, and Elkins thought it was beneficial to whatever their current plan might be. To organize Portland's vice industry, however, the Seattle group required more than threats and pickets. A corrupt public official is a necessary element in all successful criminal operations and William Langley, a Portland lawyer who, in 1954, was seeking the Democratic nomination for Multnomah County district attorney, fit the bill.

James Elkins and Teamsters union Secretary-Treasurer John Sweeney met several times in the early 1950s to discuss Portland politics. Elkins later recalled, "I asked John Sweeney why he was romancing a man in my business and he said, 'Well, no particular reason,' only he liked to be friends with people in my type of business, that the Teamsters was a powerful organization politically, and he understood I had put up quite a bit of money politically now and then and there wasn't any use of wasting it, that we could reach some kind of an agreement on it."[43] In 1954, according to Elkins, Teamsters union official Clyde Crosby asked him to set up a meeting with William Langley. Langley later admitted, however, that he initiated contact with Teamsters officials to ask for the union's support in his bid for the district attorney's office.[44]

William Langley was a native Portlander, born in March 1916, and the son of former Multnomah County District Attorney Lotus Langley. In 1938, William graduated from Northwestern College of Law in Portland, and four years later, he was hired as an assistant U.S. attorney for Oregon, a position he held until 1946.[45] Shortly after leaving his post in the U.S. attorney's office, Langley purchased the China Lantern, a nightclub located in nearby Beaverton. According to the *Oregonian*, the China Lantern (formerly known as Lambert's Drive-in) was a front for a gambling den and was part of Elkins's crime syndicate. State documents show that Langley dissolved his partnership with Elkins and madam Gerry Rogers and disposed of the property in 1949 before making his losing bid for the district attorney seat the following year. John B. McCourt won the 1950 election with support from the Teamsters union. By the 1954 election, however, McCourt had lost the backing of the Teamsters when, in support of Mayor Lee's ill-fated reforms, he publicly threatened to raid the sites of slot and pinball machines in the city.[46]

In the fall of 1954, Crosby, Sweeney, and Elkins met with Langley at the Portland airport to discuss what advantages the Teamsters and racketeers could hope to expect in return for supporting Langley's candidacy. Elkins's main demands were for prior notice when a warrant was issued to raid his gambling joints and assurance that Langley would not enforce a state law that required the padlocking of a building if there were two arrests for gambling or other vice on the premises. The Teamsters, for their part, wanted protection for Maloney's new gambling operations and cooperation from local law enforcement agencies during the union's strikes and boycotts.[47]

With all the parties in agreement, a deal was struck. Fulfilling the Teamsters' end of the bargain, Thomas Maloney traveled to Portland to take an active part in Langley's campaign. Langley knew well who he was dealing with and took a liking to him. According to Langley, Maloney was "a great big, good natured, sort of person" and "represented Frank Brewster."[48] By the end of Langley's successful campaign, Elkins reportedly paid Maloney $3,600 for helping with the election and gave Langley $1,800 for campaign materials. To Teamster Frank Malloy and his wife, Elkins paid an additional $400, while giving a variety of gifts to other Teamsters involved in organizing votes for Langley. The Teamsters' representatives, moreover, allegedly treated the new district attorney and his family to a vacation following the difficult campaign.[49]

Now it was the new district attorney's turn to make good on his end of the bargain. Shortly after the election, Teamsters Frank Brewster and John Sweeney called Elkins and Langley to Seattle to discuss what illegal activities the district attorney would allow in Portland once he took over as chief prosecutor. According to Elkins, Maloney moved to the Rose City to direct those vice operations that the district attorney agreed to allow by the terms of their pre-election bargain. Langley later told state investigators that he hired Maloney simply as an informant. Meanwhile, Brewster ordered Joseph McLaughlin to serve as the middleman between Langley, the racketeers, and Teamsters officials.[50] In return for protection against arrest and prosecution, the Seattle group ordered Elkins to pay District Attorney Langley $2,000 each month, and to cover many of Maloney's and McLaughlin's bills. Ultimately, this demand convinced Elkins to reconsider his relationship with the Seattle group. On one occasion, Elkins later testified, Langley received a $500 bonus for allowing the unmolested operation of two brothels that were connected to Maloney.[51]

Although it appears that Langley was paid for his involvement in Portland's vice operations, other Oregon politicians were simply asked to return a favor in exchange for union support at the polls. Contrary to the belief that all labor consistently backed Democrats, the Teamsters were not political partisans: Republicans could be bought and paid for just as easily as Democrats. Just as local Teamsters helped Langley, a Democrat, win the district attorney's post in 1954, the union helped Republican Paul Patterson win the governor's race. According to Howard Morgan, former chair of the Oregon State Democratic Party and a public utility commissioner, most of Oregon's labor unions supported the Democratic candidate, Joe Carson, despite Carson's anti-union stance during a tumultuous Longshoremen's strike of 1934. Yet, the Teamsters threw their support behind Patterson. According to Frank Brewster, the decision to back certain candidates in local elections was "made at the local level"; he "never attempted to influence [the local memberships'] choice."[52] Howard Morgan later testified, however, that Clyde Crosby told him that the "decision was made in Seattle to back Patterson," an indication, Morgan believed, that Teamsters union officials pushed candidates for personal reasons rather than for the good of Oregon labor.[53]

It took less than a year for Teamsters officials to call on the newly elected Republican Governor Patterson to help whitewash a state investigation of graft in the state's liquor commission. The Oregon Liquor Control Commission was created four days after Prohibition was repealed nationally in 1933. Reformist Oregonians voted to ban the sale of alcoholic beverages four years before the national ban was passed, thus with the repeal, Oregonians wanted strict guidelines to extend the progressive reform. The state, therefore, controlled the sale and distribution of all liquor; consequently, there were opportunities within this system for corruption. According to Morgan and James Elkins, Oregon Liquor Control Commissioner Thomas Sheridan received a bribe from Teamsters' representatives to support specific liquor and gambling operations.[54] Morgan explained that certain union officials wanted someone on the state liquor commission. He later testified, "Because they had bargaining disputes and membership disputes with certain distilleries in the East . . . [they] wanted to arrange whereby they could prevent liquor from certain distilleries being purchased and sold within a monopoly state like Oregon, not a drop within the boundaries, until a particular distillery signed up with the Teamsters."[55] Because the state controlled liquor sales and distribution, a liquor commissioner was a powerful figure with the authority to prevent the purchase of liquor from certain distilleries. Manton Spear, who was once the Portland representative for Seattle's K & L Distributing company, corroborated Morgan's testimony. (Coincidentally, the son of Teamsters union President Dave Beck, Dave Jr., owned K & L Distributing.) Sheridan later stated that when he was discharged in September 1955 from the Oregon Liquor Control Commission for "accepting gratuities," he contacted Portland crime boss James Elkins, who took him to see the well-connected Oregon Teamsters official Clyde Crosby.[56] Apparently, having consulted with Crosby, Thomas Maloney telephoned Sheridan a few days later and promised the distraught commissioner that he would "have Clyde talk to the governor and the governor will straighten the whole goddamned thing around."[57] Crosby also called John Sweeney in Seattle to discuss how Governor Patterson could be of service. Sweeney allegedly said, "We might as well see if we've bought a pig in the poke or if he'll perform for us," and then reportedly set up a meeting between Crosby and the governor. Within days Sheridan was reinstated with only a month's salary lost.[58] Governor Patterson also provided another useful service for Sheridan by refusing to allow Oregon's Democrat Attorney General Robert Thornton to investigate the liquor commissioner. The case was assigned instead to Multnomah County District Attorney William Langley. Knowing full well what was expected of him, the district attorney subsequently whitewashed the investigation.[59]

By the time state officials were investigating the Sheridan bribery case, James Elkins was on the outs with the Seattle group. The Portland vice racketeer believed that the group and District Attorney Langley were preparing to take control of the city's vice industry and push him out, essentially double-crossing Portland's "vice czar." To determine if this in fact was true, Elkins launched a plan that had an impact on both local and national law enforcement, labor relations, and politics. In August 1955, Elkins persuaded Maloney to move into an apartment in Portland's King Tower and, with the help of his employee, a former vice cop named Raymond Clark, Elkins installed microphones in the apartment's kitchen, living room, and telephone, and wired them to a recording machine in the adjacent apartment. Elkins also recorded his own personal conversations with the group, hoping to use the conversations as leverage. Elkins later claimed that he also used a recording device concealed in his watch. Elkins later described how, during one of his conversations with Maloney, the watch face suddenly popped off, exposing the wires attached to the recorder. Maloney looked curiously at the watch, but Elkins calmly explained that it was a new model that operated with a battery. Elkins then gathered the components and put them back into the casing.[60]

Elkins's audio recordings revealed, as he suspected, that he was going to be cut out of the action. "We should get rid of the Character [Elkins]," he heard District Attorney Langley tell Maloney and McLaughlin. "He's cheated me and he's horsing you guys around."[61] The so-called King Tower tapes are the most damning evidence of the collusion that took place between District Attorney Langley and the vice racketeers. Confronted with this irrefutable evidence, Thomas Maloney was later forced to admit to *Oregon Journal* reporter Brad Williams that he "discussed punchboards, cardrooms, and other similar operations with Joe [McLaughlin] and the Kid [William Langley]"[62] The recordings included conversations involving up to fifty people, including Maloney, McLaughlin, Oregon Liquor Control Commissioner Thomas Sheridan, and District Attorney Langley. They discussed, among other things, organizing the city's vice rackets, who was getting paid off, which Teamsters officials were involved, the Oregon Liquor Control Commission bribery case, and, of course, their plans for Elkins.[63]

From August to September 1955, Elkins collected several hours of tape-recorded conversations that he later would use to double-cross Langley and the Teamsters. At the end of September, for example, he recorded conversations surrounding District Attorney Langley's grand jury to investigate the charges that Thomas Sheridan accepted a bribe from Teamsters union officials. Thomas Maloney promised Sheridan that he would convince Langley to call the commissioner as his first witness in order to "set the record straight" from the beginning. Maloney's plan was that after all the witnesses testified, Langley could then call Sheridan to "explain inconsistencies." Maloney also explained that he would persuade certain grand jury witnesses to "go fishing"—to leave Portland—and that "Bill [Langley] will take care of the evidence."[64]

The King Tower tapes also reveal that during the grand jury investigation the district attorney sought racketeer Joseph McLaughlin's advice on how to protect Thomas Sheridan. Langley and McLaughlin together created a plan to meet with the state's chief witness, an informant for Oregon State Attorney General Robert Thornton, before he testified against Sheridan. Their plan was not so much to prep the witness, as to find out what he knew before surprising the conspirators on the stand.[65] Thornton's informant had evidence that Helen Smalley, operator of the Knotty Pine Tavern on Southwest Washington Street, paid Sheridan and another liquor commissioner $2,000 to support her liquor license.[66] Smalley, incidentally, opened and operated brothels and taverns in Portland for Thomas Maloney and the Seattle group.

Meanwhile, in a sworn deposition, another informant for the attorney general testified that "the police officers on the beat are receiving $10 . . . and that individuals on up the line are receiving larger amounts."[67] Once Attorney General Thornton got wind of this, Langley told Maloney at the King Tower apartments (where he was being recorded), "he'll be clear off the liquor commission—he'll be investigating the police department."[68] Maloney and Langley both understood that an investigation of Portland's law enforcement practices would produce evidence that Elkins and the Seattle group paid police officers and the district attorney to allow prostitution and gambling to run unmolested. Thus, they needed Thornton to stay at the capital in Salem during the grand jury investigation.

For this, they turned to Thomas Maloney. At a party in December 1955, Maloney reportedly ordered Democratic Party Chairman Howard Morgan to pass a message to the state's attorney general. Morgan later testified:

> With a cigar between his first two fingers, [Maloney] thumped me on the chest, scattering cigar ashes all over a dark blue suit I had on, and said, "You make [Attorney General Robert] Thornton lay off that liquor commission investigation," in a very loud

voice. Of course, I was angry. "That sounds like an order," and he said, "That's an order." I then told him to go to hell, but the immediate question I then told him was, "What is your interest in the liquor control commission? Why don't you want that investigated? Why do you care whether it is investigated?" He said, "You know damn well what this means to us."[69]

Later, having been informed about this conversation, Clyde Crosby rhetorically asked Morgan: "Has Maloney been trying to give you a bad time? Well, I would put it a little differently, but it amounts to the same thing. We wish Thornton would lay off."[70] Morgan evidently relayed the message to the attorney general, who decided to let District Attorney Langley handle the grand jury investigation.

With the state attorney general now off the case, racketeers Maloney and McLaughlin took control of the grand jury investigation, telling the district attorney exactly how to run it. When Thomas Sheridan complained to Maloney that certain witnesses were "weak" and that others were not in the grand jury room long enough, Maloney responded by explaining that was the strategy: "Well, Bill [Langley] made it that way."[71] There was no doubt, claimed Howard Morgan, that not only had Langley "whitewashed" the investigation, but that "an attempt was being made to take over law enforcement" in the state, in Multnomah County, and in Portland.[72] After the last witness was called to testify, Maloney telephoned Langley and told him to assure Sheridan that "he doesn't have to worry about anything."[73] Thanks to the efforts of Maloney, McLaughlin, and Langley, the grand jury did not indict Thomas Sheridan, despite overwhelming evidence that he strongly encouraged the state to purchase liquor from Teamsters union–friendly distilleries and accepted a bribe from Teamsters representatives to ignore liquor license violations at gambling establishments in Portland.

Dorothy McCullough Lee's successor, Republican Mayor Fred Peterson, found himself in the middle of this feud between Elkins and the Teamsters. The Seattle group and James Elkins both looked to Mayor Peterson as someone they could count on to support their criminal interests in Portland. A pharmacist and drugstore owner in the Hollywood district, Peterson took his landslide election over Dorothy McCullough Lee in 1952 as a mandate to reject municipal reform. Historian Carl Abbott concludes that Peterson had "an iron determination to undo the work of the previous administration" and allowed the torch of civic reform to burn out.[74] During his campaign for city council and then for the mayor's office, Fred Peterson received campaign funds from James Elkins and the Teamsters. City Commissioner Stanley Earl later explained that "Mayor Peterson had been very close with the Teamsters union and pin ball [sic] people."[75]

Mayor Peterson made many questionable decisions and dubious appointments. For example, in 1953, Portlanders approved an $8 million bond to build an arena for live entertainment and sporting events to be named the Exposition-Recreation Center, later renamed Memorial Coliseum. The site chosen for the arena also played a role in the Elkins–Teamsters union feud. Before the bond was even approved, Mayor Peterson appointed an Exposition-Recreation Commission, a five-man panel of city leaders with the authority to select the location for the planned arena. Two of the appointees to the commission, however, had questionable and controversial backgrounds. One of Peterson's questionable selections was James Polhemus, the president of Portland General Electric. At one time the general manager of the Port of Portland, Polhemus had been accused in the 1930s of using his position for personal financial gain. Polhemus allegedly offered special treatment to friends in the shipping and distribution industries. Subsequently, Frank Akin, the independent auditor who discovered Polhemus's financial discrepancies, was found murdered on November 20, 1933. The murder is still unsolved, but it seems that he was killed to protect Polhemus and his friends.[76] The other controversial appointee to the Exposition-Recreation Commission was Teamsters official Clyde Crosby.

Speaking to his appointed commissioners, Mayor Peterson asserted, "It is your obligation and yours alone to determine the location of this facility," whereupon the commission hired the Stanford Research Institute to survey possible arena locations.[77] Potential investors hoped that the commission would choose the "underutilized blocks" downtown, south of Portland's Civic (now Keller) Auditorium. While Portland voters ultimately decided the project location, their choices were limited to either the southwest Portland location or a site on the east side of the Willamette River. In May 1956, and again in November to confirm their choice, voters chose the east side location.[78]

The site selection was not entirely unexpected. In early 1955, Crosby met with James Elkins in the Teamster's office in Portland. Spread out over Crosby's desk was a large map highlighting the potential sites for the planned sports arena. While discussing the Stanford study, and the possibility that Crosby could influence the selection of the east side Broadway-Steel Bridge site, Crosby ordered Elkins to buy property around the proposed location. While Maloney and McLaughlin gave Elkins a portion of the $340,000 needed for the acquisition, Crosby lobbied heavily for the site, knowing that the city would need to purchase the surrounding area to meet the requirement of the construction plan.[79]

Crosby proposed Exposition-Recreation Commission Resolution 30, which sponsored the Broadway-Steel Bridge site.[80] Meanwhile, Elkins and Seattle racketeer Joseph McLaughlin set out to purchase the options to certain properties. Realtor John Kelley of John Kelley and Sons reported that Elkins and McLaughlin visited his office in January 1955 to inquire about property in the Williams Avenue area. Elkins and McLaughlin then returned in April or May 1955 and purchased the options.[81] Kelley claimed he "received an inkling" that the two men had information about the property because Elkins told him they had a friend who had an "in." Kelley later testified that Clyde Crosby was mentioned "on at least six occasions and, at one point, when a question of the extension of the area to be acquired came up, McLaughlin stated that he wanted to use the phone to call Crosby."[82] Kelley continued, "It is my belief that McLaughlin called because, apparently, Jim Elkins, who was paying for the options and, for that matter, this whole venture, wanted to be sure that before he paid for any further options on the extended area, he would receive some assurance that this area would be profitable in the Exposition-Recreation venture. It is my best recollection that the total gross options held by Elkins, McLaughlin, and [Tom] Johnson was about a half million dollars."[83] Abbott suggests that the decision to locate the arena in the Broadway-Steel Bridge area "had the side effects of clearing the southern end of Portland's black neighborhood and increasing the attractiveness of Lloyd Corporation land around the new Lloyd Center shopping complex. More generally, the ad hoc format for the decision invited special interests to set the agenda."[84] It is now known that businessmen operating in both legal and illegal industries were interested in the east side location and that Tom Johnson, a racketeer and former bootlegger, owned most of the real estate Elkins and McLaughlin were ordered to secure.[85]

According to Elkins, McLaughlin later told him that Teamsters officials John Sweeney and Frank Brewster were unhappy about Crosby's scheme because it took the group's attention away from organizing Portland's vice rackets. Sweeney and Brewster told Crosby, however, that they would let the matter rest for one-third of the take. While the site for the sports arena was chosen by the Exposition-Recreation Commission, Elkins killed the deal by failing to deliver the deeds. He apparently purchased the options to the land, but hearing of Brewster's disapproval, anxious over the deal struck with Crosby, McLaughlin, and Maloney, and now believing that he was to be cut out of the group's larger plans for Portland's vice operations, Elkins let the options run out. Crosby, fuming over the $340,000 loss, felt more pressure from Seattle, where he was criticized both for his involvement in the scheme and for the failure of the vice rackets in Portland to produce the revenues that Sweeney and Brewster expected.[86]

By late 1955, the Seattle group's plan to take over Portland's lucrative vice industry began to unravel. The business relationship between James Elkins, Teamsters officials, and the Seattle racketeers ended when, according to Elkins, Thomas Maloney suggested opening three or four brothels and establishing an illegal abortion ring. Maloney arranged a meeting at the Heathman Hotel between Elkins and Ann Thompson, a successful Seattle madam, who later testified that Elkins had become uneasy about becoming involved in prostitution. Elkins said that he "drew the line" at operating brothels, having "never been involved" in prostitution, a claim that was contradicted later by several reports. "He just discouraged me and talked me out of it," Thompson later testified. Soon afterward, Maloney arranged for a meeting between Elkins and Seattle mobster Frank Colacurcio, who "wanted me [Elkins] to arrange so that he could take over three or four houses [of prostitution]." Elkins remembered: "I told him if he wanted the houses to go buy them." The two did not reach an agreement and Colacurcio went back to Seattle.[87]

Prostitution was not the only thing that came between Elkins and his partners. Elkins believed that Maloney, McLaughlin, Brewster, and Crosby were putting too much pressure on him to open more gambling properties. *Oregonian* reporter William Lambert recalled listening to the King Tower tapes and hearing District Attorney William Langley telling Thomas Maloney "what they were going to [do] . . . to the 'Character' they called Elkins, and how they were going to do it. They were going to cut him out. . . . 'This Character is giving us a bad time.'"[88] From the tapes, Elkins learned that he was the target of the group's animosity. Langley explained that they needed to "get rid of Elkins." "Well, tell him [Elkins] I want my eighty-five hundred when you talk to him," Langley demanded. "You can tell him that too. The son of a bitch, he—you guys can have the eighty-five hundred, ha, I don't want it, but I don't want that dizzy bastard acting the way he's acting."[89]

Clyde Crosby also complained that he did not receive his cut of the profits from Maloney and McLaughlin, and that Brewster was angry. "I am going to tell you something," Elkins claimed Brewster threatened, "I make mayors and I break mayors, and I make chiefs of police and I break chiefs of police. I have been in jail and I have been out of jail . . . nothing scares me. If you bother my two boys, if you embarrass my two boys, you will find yourself wading across Lake Washington with a pair of concrete boots."[90] Elkins was afraid of the Teamsters and realized that they might kill him. Earlier that year, in fact, Elkins told Frank Brewster that he wanted out of their partnership in Portland.

Yet, Elkins was hardly a "reluctant" partner; he was more than willing to allow the Seattle group to enter into Portland's vice industry in exchange for his control over a few gambling machines in the Portland Labor Temple, as well as the district attorney's protection from law enforcement. Elkins clearly cooperated with the Seattle group and District Attorney Langley. Nonetheless, to give himself a stronger position from which he could resist the Teamsters and regain his stronghold on the city's vice rackets, Elkins launched the second phase of his plan to double-cross the Seattle group. Elkins used the news media, which, in the spirit of the great Progressive Era muckrakers, had the ability to pressure city leaders to crack down on any union attempt to control Portland's political machinery and vice industry.

Progressive Era union organizers fought for the right to organize and bargain collectively for simple demands, such as higher wages, safer working conditions, and more leisure time. The postwar Teamsters leaders, particularly Dave Beck, Frank Brewster, and Jimmy Hoffa, molded the union into a force that intimidated business, political, and other labor leaders, and engaged in organized crime; with help from Seattle vice racketeers, the Teamsters were closing in on James Elkins's vice rackets in Portland. Meanwhile, there were reports in Detroit, New York, and Chicago that law enforcement officers, vice racketeers, and corrupt labor leaders cooperated to successfully organize criminal operations in those cities. The Rose City is central to the history of crime and corruption in American cities. In fact, federal authorities in 1956 determined that the Portland case was vital to their nationwide investigation and effort to eliminate organized crime, political corruption, and labor racketeering in America.

FOUR

THE PORTLAND
VICE SCANDAL

REALIZING THE IMPACT THAT THE SEATTLE RACKETEERS AND
Teamsters union officials would have on his vice rackets in Portland,
and considering the violent threat issued by Teamsters' chief Frank
Brewster, James Elkins concluded that he had very few options to
protect his properties and his life. Elkins's tried and true methods
of running his competition out of Portland would not work against
this group. To ensure his survival in an increasingly hostile climate,
he decided to go to the press with his sensational story of organized
crime, law enforcement corruption, and labor racketeering. The
opportunity came when *Oregonian* investigative reporter Wallace
Turner contacted Elkins in February 1956 to ask him if there was
any truth to the rumors that a candidate for mayor in the upcoming
election was involved in the city's vice rackets.[1] While Elkins denied
the rumors, his contact with Turner opened the door to telling the
reporter about his troubles—that the Seattle group planned to connect the Portland and Seattle crime syndicates, and that if he got in
the way, they would likely kill him. Elkins eventually gave Turner
and his partner, William Lambert, irrefutable evidence—the King
Tower tapes—that linked Portland's district attorney and other law

enforcement officials to the city's criminal underground and corrupt Teamsters union officials.[2]

The reports of backroom gambling, prostitution rings, municipal graft, and corrupt union leadership made for sensational reading when first published in the local and then in the national newspapers and magazines between 1956 and 1960.[3] These reports came after decades of crime and corruption had plagued the Rose City, and Portland was not unique, but is a perfect example of crime and corruption that plagued many American cities during the twentieth century. Critics argued at the time, and skeptics argue today, that the *Oregonian* reporters did not conclusively prove the charges of corruption because they relied on Elkins—a convicted felon and kingpin of the local vice rackets—and mostly lacked corroboration. In fact, by 1957, 115 grand jury indictments had been filed by Oregon's attorney general against forty-one defendants, including Seattle racketeers Thomas Maloney and Joseph McLaughlin, Portland Teamsters official Clyde Crosby, Multnomah County District Attorney William Langley, Portland Police Chief James Purcell, and "vice czar" James Elkins.

Elkins's role in Portland's criminal underworld was absent from the initial *Oregonian* newspaper coverage. In August 2003, journalist Wallace Turner explained that he omitted Elkins and his operations from his articles in exchange for information on organized crime, including vice, narcotics, and police graft. Turner recalled that Elkins "understood that his role was to attempt to supply credible information when asked. Our side of the arrangement . . . was to let him alone in minor matters, and for my part, not to initiate stories that would lead the police to raid his after-hours joints."[4]

Turner later said that he benefited from contacts with numerous sources, not only in Portland, but throughout Oregon and Washington. They told him of local and state politics mixed with crime, which he duly reported and which put Turner squarely in the path of bribes. "I began to be offered money [as I] began to see that there were gambling joints going, liquor by the drink [being served]," which was illegal in Oregon. Turner later insisted, "I was not for sale." Elkins first tried to bribe the journalist in 1948 because the newspaper reports on vice activities were causing him trouble with the city's law enforcement agencies. "I got a call one day from Jim Elkins," Turner remembered, and as the reporter was later leaving city hall, Elkins pulled up in a blue convertible Buick and offered him $500. "I remember telling him . . . as I rejected his $500, 'I don't take money. I take information.'" In 1956, Elkins offered Turner and Lambert wrist watches. This bribe attempt amused the two reporters.[5]

The relationship between Elkins and the reporters was no different from that of a police officer and an informant. In exchange for useful information, officers often overlook lesser criminal offenses. Turner, though, was not responsible for policing Elkins's actions, nor was he an official guardian of public morality. For several months, he was able to use the racketeer's information to alert the public to greater, possibly more destructive operations, and, as Turner seemed to suggest, aid law enforcement officials in identifying the real "bad guys."[6] Turner, described by *Time* magazine as "gangling" and "sharp-nosed," and his partner William Lambert, with his thick eye-glasses, hardly seemed the types to insert themselves into the Portland vice network, but "Fishface" and "Bugeyes," as they were known to the local underworld, were pivotal in bringing the city's underground dealings to light.[7]

When Turner contacted Elkins in February 1956 to investigate mayoral candidate Joe Dobbins's connections to Portland's vice industry, Turner did not know what he was getting into. *Oregonian* publisher Mike Frey had heard the Dobbins rumor and, concerned that "a bad guy" was running for mayor, asked Turner to look into it. "It seemed to me at the time," Turner later explained, "that a sense of duty guided [editors Mike Frey and Robert Notson]. Then, the story was one that any real newspaperman could not ignore."[8]

In a wide sweep of his informants, Turner recalled, he came to Elkins and arranged a meeting.[9] Up Broadway Avenue from the

Oregonian Building, Turner and Elkins parked along the curb in the racketeer's blue convertible. Discussing the rumors swirling about the mayoral candidate, Elkins explained that Dobbins was "just a car dealer" (which was his legitimate job).[10] Then Turner got out of the car and turned to Elkins. "You look bad," Turner said. "You been sick?" "No," Elkins answered, "been . . . fightin' with the Teamsters."[11] Elkins then told Turner that the Seattle mobsters had threatened to frame him on a felony charge or kill him for botching a land deal, involving the Exposition-Recreation site, and for backing out of plans to link the Portland and Seattle crime syndicates. Elkins also told Turner about the Seattle group's relationship with Portland's district attorney, William Langley.[12] Turner later clarified, "I think people believe he [Elkins] burbled this out to this old friend Wally. We were not friends. We tried hard to use each other; from time to time we found common ground. He knew I could write news stories that would cause him lots of trouble. . . . He talked to us only because he had no place left to go. Of course, he hoped to drive out the other guys, but I knew, and told him, that he was through when we published what he was telling us. He believed he could maneuver his way through."[13]

This meeting was a critical turning point in the relationship that had developed between the reporters and the racketeer. According to Turner, shortly after their discussion in the convertible, Elkins delivered the King Tower tapes to him and the *Oregonian*. William Lambert later explained, "I think when Wally (Turner) went out that day to talk to him that Elkins had probably just about come to the point where he figured maybe I'd better tell somebody on the newspaper about this."[14] After listening to seventy hours of taped conversations, Turner and Lambert spent three months double-checking their data and Elkins's claims, which included trips to San Francisco and Seattle. Meanwhile, the reporters moved out of the *Oregonian* building and across Columbia Avenue into the New Hungerford Hotel in order to interview "our hoodlum sources," Turner later remembered, as well as for their own protection.[15]

The King Tower tapes clearly revealed that District Attorney Langley accepted bribes to protect certain operations and threatened many vice operators with abatement if they did not pay him. Wallace Turner vividly recalled the tape excerpts of District Attorney Langley counting money he received from a gambling operator.[16] Explaining a payoff from a vice operator who was running three gambling dens, Langley said, "Well, now he gave me something for the two, $450. . . . He gave me $200 for each one of the Chinamen [gambling operators] and $50 was for the Big Seven [gambling den]."[17] Langley also clearly supported the Seattle group's operation of vice properties in Portland, as in this exchange with Joseph McLaughlin, who led the McKinley crime family in Seattle:

LANGLEY: Well, you oughta get yourself going. How many . . . how many games have we got going in there? Just one?

MCLAUGHLIN: You know that joint's been going for some time and I tell you it takes time.

LANGLEY: How about the high dice? Tom . . . Tom [Maloney] was talking about the high dice. Are you going to put that in?

MCLAUGHLIN: No, I don't know why, they were going [to] but they didn't . . .

LANGLEY: And, uh, you see now, Tom told me that you want to go open up some kind of a book. Is that right?

MCLAUGHLIN: Well, that's not unless there's a safe way.

LANGLEY: If you can get a book goin' and get some poker games goin', Tom oughta be able to make enough money. . . . Now, he's just down to cards or craps or whores. Well, I've committed myself on whores and I can't back up right on that . . . or I look bad. Well, you can't run a huckley-buck craps game— that's out of the question, so you're right back to cards, but he's gonna have to have a whole lot of poker games goin' in order to make it big.[18]

Of course, the conspirators realized that audio recordings of their conversations with District Attorney Langley could be very damaging. As McLaughlin told Maloney:

> It's a very dangerous thing for the Kid [Langley], if anything leaks on out. . . . He could be recalled and knocked on out of there. So don't allow him to talk on the phone. If there is anything he wants to tell you in regards to anything, you gotta meet him. If they did get a recording . . . it would blow up higher than a kite and [he could] possibly [be] sent away. . . . It would ruin the man the rest of his life; and for a bootleg joint or anything else, it isn't worth a thing.[19]

Around the second week in April 1956, senior editors at the *Oregonian* contacted Oregon governor and former newspaper publisher Elmo Smith to give him a "heads up" on the damning evidence they were compiling and the story they planned to publish. The governor was already familiar with the Teamsters. As a state senator from eastern Oregon, Smith sponsored and secured the passage of a weight-mile tax for Oregon highways, a law opposed by the trucking industry.[20] According to Oregon's attorney general, Robert Thornton, the governor sent his assistant, Ed Armstrong, and two state police officials to meet with the *Oregonian* editors and listen to the King Tower tapes. Thornton later criticized the Republican governor for playing party politics in his decision to not give the attorney general the evidence uncovered by the *Oregonian* reporters. Thornton was a Democrat running for re-election against a Republican nominee. Because Governor Smith was cautious and did not send the case immediately to Thornton, the attorney general concluded that the governor authorized the newspapermen to print their story.[21]

On April 19, 1956, the *Oregonian* launched the first article of Turner and Lambert's investigation. Titled "City, County Control Sought by Gangsters," the article described the plan initiated by the Seattle racketeers and Teamsters union officials to take over law enforcement in Portland and to dominate the city's vice industry.[22] What made the story even more sensational was its implication of the Multnomah County district attorney. The series continued for a week, during which Turner and Lambert described in vivid detail Portland's record of organized crime, municipal corruption, and labor racketeering in articles headlined, "Top Teamster Seeks Police Chief Ouster," "Profit Making Pact Tied to E-R Center Options," and "District Attorney Close to Gambler Group."[23] Among the more lurid storylines was how Teamsters official Clyde Crosby and racketeer Thomas Maloney pressured Portland Mayor Fred Peterson to replace Police Chief James Purcell because the chief periodically raided Thomas Maloney's gambling operations, despite Purcell's cooperation with James Elkins. The series also documented Crosby's sports arena scheme and quoted from the taped conversations of Langley, McLaughlin, Maloney, Oregon Liquor Control Commissioner Sheridan, and others involved in Portland's vice industry. The article titled "Seattle Men, Prosecutor Confer Often," characterized District Attorney Langley's "intimate" relationship with the Seattle racketeers and Teamsters union leaders."[24]

Although no public announcement was made to this effect, Turner and Lambert "more or less withdrew" from their coverage of the story after the initial series. As Turner later explained, "I knew from past experience [that] we would quickly be targets of those we accused. That made us a part of the story so it was improper for us to try to cover it."[25] Therefore, the coverage of the scandal was reassigned to various *Oregonian* journalists who submitted reports describing the impact of the exposé and subsequent investigations.

As a consequence of Turner and Lambert's articles, the *Oregonian* faced lawsuits totaling $3.6 million, all of which were later dismissed. The series earned the newspaper a Pulitzer Prize in 1957 and the reporters were awarded the American Newspaper Guild's Heywood Broun Award for journalistic excellence. *Time* magazine suggested that the *Oregonian*'s exposé was inspirational; the magazine's editors characterized the *Oregonian* as a "comfortable, conservative newspaper that is normally inclined to sit back and rock on Portland's front porch," but acknowledged that this exposé was "tough and hazardous" reporting.[26] While the muckrakers of the Progressive Era, like Ida Tarbell, were well-known for their courage in their fight for reform, journalists in the 1950s, with notable exceptions like Edward R. Murrow, seldom bucked consensus restraints. Not until Woodward and Bernstein in 1972 would newspaper reporters risk as much as Turner and Lambert in their exposure of Portland's corrupt officials.

On April 20, 1956, the day after the first *Oregonian* article appeared, Governor Smith contacted District Attorney Langley, Assistant District Attorney Howard Lonergan, and state law enforcement officials to discuss the allegations. After a four-hour conference at the capitol, Langley told the assembled reporters in Salem that allegations that he plotted with the Teamsters were false, but that he did not doubt that "thugs in the Teamsters union might have tried to move in on Elkins."[27] While he admitted to having been endorsed by the union in 1954, Langley claimed that he had "never taken a cent from them and [had] not seen any of their officials in months."[28] The district attorney contended that a fight between "thug and thug" for control of Portland's vice industry propelled him into the scandal; yet, he remained unsullied by his "refusal to bow to either one of the underworld elements."[29]

Following the conference in Salem, District Attorney Langley returned to Portland where he convinced the editors of the *Oregon Journal*, the *Oregonian*'s competitor, that a "Portland underworld czar" ordered the city police to wiretap his phone and collect blackmail information on city officials. In its attempt to provide fair and balanced coverage of the scandal, the *Journal* allowed Langley to answer the allegations by publishing his response. In his retort, the district attorney denied his involvement with racketeers Joseph McLaughlin and Thomas Maloney, and he insisted that Elkins's "squabble" with the Teamsters was the basis for the "current excitement." In addition, Langley accused Mayor Fred Peterson, Police

Chief Purcell, and Elkins of forming an "unholy alliance" to discredit him.[30] Langley told reporters that a "police official" (that is, Chief Purcell) was "taking orders" from Elkins and was protecting the racketeer's criminal operations. On April 19, 1956, in response to the first *Oregonian* story, Langley proclaimed to reporters, "I have evidence that Elkins has been a frequent visitor to the office of Purcell. I also have evidence that Purcell and Elkins have met quietly in a large, green Chrysler convertible on side streets."[31]

William Langley received his information from a spy who connected Police Chief James Purcell and Mayor Fred Peterson to clubs running gambling games and hotels associated with prostitution. This spy, later identified as gambler Leo Plotkins, told Langley that the police chief and mayor sheltered these establishments from law enforcement. Racketeer Joseph McLaughlin advised that this bit of information could be used for "protection and insurance" against Chief Purcell, who "doesn't want to be put out and pushed on out."

> MCLAUGHLIN: Show that you've been gathering, trying to get all this evidence and the like in regards to this stuff. So it's just protection for you.
>
> LANGLEY: I can threaten Peterson. . . . I won't hesitate if that spy tells me one of 'em [is] going. I'm going to call up Peterson and tell him: "What do you want, a grand jury investigation here over prostitution like [Attorney General] Thornton had over the liquor commission?" . . . Well do you think the reason they want the sporting houses to go and nothing else is because they got leases on the buildings?
>
> MCLAUGHLIN: That's right."[32]

The accusations against Chief Purcell were not unfounded. According to an Oregon State Police informant, Purcell was in the pocket of James Elkins, who paid Mayor Peterson $100,000 to appoint his man chief of the police bureau. As a police officer, James Purcell had a reputation for being friendly to the city's after-hours clubs and had at one time been a co-owner of the Penguin Club, a gambling establishment off Sandy Boulevard. After his appointment as chief of police, Purcell allegedly lowered the Penguin Club's monthly payoff to the police bureau.[33] When the Seattle group began to move into Portland's rackets, however, Chief Purcell would not cooperate because of his close association with Elkins.

Perhaps Chief Purcell wanted a bigger payoff for himself than the group was willing to pay. "Now supposin', uh, now supposin' you get rid of Purcell," Langley proposed to McLaughlin in August 1955, "and get, and get what's-his-name in there, this Dave . . . it's gonna be better off if he's [Purcell] not gonna go on this 100 percent. . . . That Jim Purcell's so goddamned hungry for money that he wouldn't even go to his dad's funeral if it meant making a few bucks. I'm telling you . . . he's a money crazy guy."[34] Setting up the rackets would have been easier for the Seattle group with James Purcell out of the way, James Elkins later admitted.[35]

Thus, the conspirators set out to get rid of Police Chief James Purcell. Thomas Maloney approached John Bardell Purcell, a former Portland vice detective, inspector for the Portland Boxing Commission, and brother of Chief James Purcell.[36] Maloney, John Bardell Purcell later claimed, "suggested I speak to my brother, Jim Purcell Jr., the chief of police, about allowing some illegal activities to operate within the city."[37] There is no evidence that John Bardell Purcell spoke to his brother, but District Attorney Langley suggested that Portland Teamsters official Clyde Crosby could convince the mayor to replace the chief of police: "Suppose that they [the Teamsters and Crosby] convinced Pete [Peterson] . . . that the labor people can't go for Pete as long as Jim Purcell is in there."[38]

In the fall of 1955, Crosby paid Mayor Peterson a visit. Peterson later admitted to the Oregon State Police that he "lunched with Crosby quite often."[39] At this particular meeting, Crosby informed the mayor that "[Seattle Teamsters' officials Frank] Brewster, [John] Sweeney, and I talked this over and I have been instructed to tell you that if Purcell continues to be chief of police, we will have to find another candidate for mayor to support."[40]

In an interview with the Oregon State Police in 1956, the mayor also admitted that Crosby introduced him to Thomas Maloney in December 1954. According to the police report, "Crosby offered the services of Maloney to him [Peterson] to act as a campaign manager. He refused the offer as he already had a campaign manager, however, he did use Maloney considerably in his campaign as he found that Maloney had many good ideas. Following the introduction of Maloney to Mayor Peterson, Maloney called at his office many times and became quite familiar with him."[41] Maloney told Mayor Peterson that Teamsters official John Sweeney ordered him to assist the mayor in his campaign just as he had for District Attorney William Langley in 1954.[42] Nevertheless, in his interview with Joseph Uris in 1980, Peterson insisted that he did not tolerate vice crime and municipal graft.[43]

Meanwhile, on April 21, 1956, two days after the *Oregonian* exposé hit newsstands, District Attorney Langley ordered a county grand jury hearing to investigate the Portland vice scandal and the newspaper's allegations. Among those subpoenaed were James Elkins and his employee Ray Clark, Teamsters official Clyde Crosby, and Seattle hoodlums Joseph McLaughlin and Thomas Maloney. Because city, county, and state officials were all implicated—specifically Mayor Fred Peterson, Police Chief James Purcell, and Multnomah County Sheriff Terry Schrunk—they were invited to testify as well. Subpoenas were also issued to reporters Wallace Turner and William Lambert, and *Oregonian* editor Herbert Lundy, but they refused to respond, claiming that Langley was trying to stop publication of further articles about the scandal. For their part, the Teamsters threatened the newspaper with a delivery driver's strike if it printed anything more about Teamsters' corruption. "All [the *Oregonian's*] got to do," Thomas Maloney explained to James Elkins, "is [word redacted] around with the Teamsters and the first thing you know them guys will be up there wanting 10 or

15 cents an hour and the *Oregonian* can't afford it. . . . So, when they can't afford it, they'll have the pickets around the ___ing joint and the ___ing paper'll lay dead still."[44]

The fact that William Langley was leading the grand jury inquiry into a case that implicated him was undoubtedly problematic. Fully aware of this conflict of interest, state Attorney General Robert Thornton immediately requested that Governor Smith put him in charge of the investigation, which the governor did on April 23, just two days after Langley ordered the grand jury hearing.[45] Governor Smith effectively shut down Langley's grand jury investigation, and from that point forward the state was in charge.[46]

District Attorney Langley continued to act as Multnomah County's chief law enforcement officer and used his authority to confiscate the King Tower tapes, which clearly implicated him in the Portland vice scandal. Reporter Wallace Turner later testified that he believed Langley seized the tapes with the intention of using them to frame James Elkins and his employee, Ray Clark, on federal wiretapping charges. On May 17, 1956, Langley and Assistant District Attorney Howard Lonergan, acting on a tip from *Oregon Journal* reporter Brad Williams, created an affidavit, which Langley signed, that stipulated a probable cause to search Clark's home for obscene pornographic photographs and sound recordings. They then delivered the affidavit to the district court judge, who in turn issued the warrant, which was then delivered to Multnomah County Sheriff Terry Schrunk.[47]

At about 8:00 p.m. on the same day, Sheriff Schrunk gave the search warrant to Deputy George Minielly, who then called for other deputies to assist him in the search. With *Oregon Journal* reporters Brad Williams, Doug Baker, and Rolla Crick following along, the deputies proceeded to Clark's home on Southeast Main Street and broke through his door. Around 10:00 p.m., Sheriff Schrunk arrived to supervise the search, and shortly thereafter, Deputy Minielly found the King Tower tapes in a hassock. "This is what I've been looking for," Minielly reportedly remarked, whereupon he put the tapes in a paper sack and locked them in his car.[48] The King Tower tapes, however, were not included in either the warrant or the inventory receipt given to Clark.[49]

The following morning, May 18, Sheriff Schrunk called Raymond Kell, his friend and lawyer, to ask if he could legally make copies of the King Tower tapes. Kell responded affirmatively, maintaining that making copies would safeguard the essential information.[50] Sheriff Schrunk subsequently allowed engineers from the radio station KPOJ (owned by the *Oregon Journal*), *Journal* reporters Brad Williams and Doug Baker, Raymond Kell, and District Attorney Langley to listen to and copy the tapes, while the originals were then entrusted to Williams and Baker for safekeeping. The next day, Williams invited Teamsters official Clyde Crosby and his wife to his home to listen to and make copies of the tapes for himself.[51]

That same day, District Attorney Langley telephoned FBI Special Agent Joseph Santoiana Jr. and described the confiscated tapes, informing the agent that the tapes consisted of "intercepted conversations" between Portland and Seattle and that since the conversations were "interstate in character" the recordings violated federal law. Santoiana asked Langley how he knew these were interstate calls; Langley replied that while he had not listened to the recordings himself, others had, and they believed that "some of the conversations were interstate." The agent then assured Langley that the FBI would monitor the local investigation and would have to hear the tapes before it could determine whether or not any federal laws were broken.[52]

Trying to steer attention away from himself and instead toward James Elkins, on May 21, District Attorney Langley, with Assistant District Attorney Howard Lonergan, requested that a state grand jury indict Clark and Elkins for violating state wiretapping laws. The indictments were quickly returned—on the heels of the May 18 search that netted the tapes—raising the question of whether the defendants had an opportunity to appeal the warrant. When a warrant's legitimacy is in question, the warrant can be appealed, thus postponing a search until a judge can rule on the case; and if a search is executed, but later ruled illegal, then anything seized is forfeited. Langley's warrant was served late on May 17, and the search followed the next morning, which also turned out to be the day of a primary election. This meant that the Multnomah County courthouse was closed until the following Monday—the warrant could not be appealed until then, leaving plenty of time for the search to be executed and for Langley, Crosby, Schrunk, and others to make copies of the King Tower tapes that they found.[53]

On May 23, Judge Walter Mears issued his ruling. The search and seizure of the tapes was illegal and the recordings were to be turned over to the Oregon State Police.[54] Numerous copies were made, but the originals were locked in a safety deposit box at First State Bank of Milwaukie, that is, until September 5, 1956, when a federal judge ordered U.S. Attorney Ed Luckey and the FBI to confiscate them. This meant that if proceedings for federal criminal violations should take place, prosecutors would have secure access to the evidence. Although Special Agent Joseph Santoiana Jr. retained the tapes, the FBI did not look into the case any further.[55]

Meanwhile, behind locked doors, Assistant District Attorney Howard Lonergan ignored the governor's order that the state take over the investigation and busied himself with the county grand jury. Oregon State Attorney General Robert Thornton later described Lonergan as "turning out indictments likety-split," in an effort to "get all of Langley's accusers put away before they could testify against Langley."[56] After many delays, Judge Alfred P. Dobson ordered the grand jury to begin hearing the state's evidence. Armed with a court order, state police officers, and his assistants, Attorney General Thornton literally forced his way into the jury chambers and took charge of the county's inquiry. He then personally led the grand jury to another room in the county courthouse.[57]

By June 1956, after many delays and distractions, Attorney General Thornton finally presented the evidence related to the Portland vice scandal. In a move that would later hamper the inquiry, the venue was changed from the county courthouse to a state office building because recording devices were discovered in the courthouse jury room.[58] Among the first to testify were *Oregonian* reporters Wallace Turner and William Lambert, and *Oregon Journal* reporter Doug Baker, who were asked to brief the jurors on all that they had compiled on Portland's corrupt municipal officials, local organized crime, and labor racketeering.[59] "This newspaper explosion," Thornton recalled, referring to the exposé, "scared quite a number of witnesses out of the jurisdiction" and made it difficult for him and his assistants to investigate the allegations.[60] Thomas Maloney, for example, fled Portland and went into hiding in Seattle and then in northern Idaho where he stayed with Seattle vice racketeer Frank Colacurcio.

Based on the reporters' allegations and conversations recorded on the King Tower tapes, Thornton also called District Attorney Langley to testify about his relationship with the Teamsters and vice racketeers. Langley refused to appear and rationalized his decision to the media by claiming, "The *Oregonian*, aided by top racketeers, has used all of its newspaper technique to smear me, including the use of phony recordings made by blackmailers and racketeers in an attempt to intimidate me." The district attorney also accused the *Oregonian* of publishing his statements "out of context, edited, and [with] libelous phrases inserted" to make it seem that he took the payoffs.[61]

After nine weeks of hearings, during which two hundred witnesses were questioned, the state grand jury concluded its investigation in August 1956. Its thirty-two indictments included charges against District Attorney Langley, Police Chief Purcell, Teamsters official Clyde Crosby, and "vice czar" James Elkins. The grand jury also found sufficient evidence to indict the Coin Machine Men of Oregon for extortion. Furthermore, local Teamsters Clyde Crosby, Frank Malloy, and Lloyd Hildreth and racketeers Elkins, McLaughlin, and Maloney were indicted for having organized the

Coin Machine Men of Oregon to control gambling machine distribution in Portland. These last indictments stated that the Teamsters "corruptly and feloniously" agreed "to conspire and confederate to threaten injury to the property of certain persons . . . with the intent to force businesses to refrain from owning, operating, buying, and selling" coin-operated machines not owned or controlled by the Coin Machine Men of Oregon. The union was charged with threatening Stanley and Gladys Terry and their pinball machine customers, which included Horace Crouch, owner of the Mount Hood Café.[62]

Perhaps one of the grand jury's most significant acts was its indictment of Clyde Crosby for extortion and conspiracy for his attempt to influence the selection of the Exposition-Recreation arena site and profit from the land surrounding the site.[63] On July 31, Sheriff Terry Schrunk took Crosby into custody following a baseball game they watched together at Sckavone Field in southeast Portland.[64]

After arresting Crosby, Sheriff Schrunk arrested District Attorney Langley, who was indicted for conspiracy to commit the felony of hindering and obstructing public justice. The jurors agreed that Langley willfully and unlawfully neglected and refused to inform against, arrest, or prosecute Multnomah County vice operators and their customers. The indictment specifically referred to Langley at a party at Jack & Jill's nightclub in March 1955 where he allegedly gambled. Langley was also indicted for extortion, as were Maloney and McLaughlin. The grand jury concluded Langley pressured Mayor Peterson in July 1955 "to permit and allow [the] operation of certain gambling games" managed by David Nance and Robert Seegar, local club operators cooperating with the Seattle group. The indictment also referred to Maloney's request that John Bardell Purcell ask his brother the police chief to overlook "certain illegal enterprises" of interest to the group.[65]

William Langley responded to these indictments by attacking the *Oregonian*. He claimed that the newspaper worked "hand-inglove" with Portland's criminal "underworld" and collaborated with "a political-minded" state's attorney general "in inferring [his] guilt." "I have been the chief obstacle," Langley charged, "to the underworld racketeers for whom the *Oregonian* has shown a special fondness in the investigation."[66] Wallace Turner later commented, "The district attorney is the 900 pound gorilla in public life because he can do whatever he damn well pleases until somebody jerks his chain."[67] Following his arraignment at the Multnomah County courthouse, the district attorney physically assaulted *Oregonian* photographer Allan DeLay and smashed his $400 camera. The photographer filed a complaint with the city police and, by the end of the day, Langley was arrested at his home with yet another charge against him.[68]

On August 3, 1956, the state grand jury indicted Police Chief Purcell for incompetence, delinquency, and malfeasance in office. The jury charged Purcell with failing to suppress illegal gambling, bootlegging, and prostitution activities; Purcell was also charged with failing to suppress graft in his police department. The indictment included the names of more than a dozen local prostitutes, gamblers, bootleggers, and vice racketeers, including James Elkins, to whom the police chief provided protection during his tenure. The chief surrendered at the county jail at 10:00 p.m. on August 3 and posted bail.[69]

The indictments of police officers Floyd Hutchins, Francis Rondhus, Robert La Fortune, Raymond Roadnight, Jack Childers, Clinton Barker, Robert Sprague, and Norman Reiter were based on evidence collected by Patrolman Jack Olsen and *Oregonian* reporter James Miller. Although Olsen had admitted receiving nearly $200 in "smile money" for "overlooking" certain gambling operations in north Portland, he was part of a plan designed by Miller and *Oregonian* executives to expose graft in Portland's Police Bureau. Once Attorney General Robert Thornton assumed control of the investigation in April, Miller and Olsen, who collected the money and recorded the serial numbers on the bills, gave state investigators a ledger indicating the bribes the officers received.[70]

Mayor Fred Peterson was badly hurt by the grand jury indictments, newspaper publicity, and the implication that his administration was soft on organized crime and acted under pressure from the Teamsters. The mayor's re-election campaign slumped as the public learned more about the administration's connections to vice and labor racketeers. Moreover, mayoral candidate Sheriff Terry Schrunk capitalized on Peterson's bad publicity. Amidst the campaign and the excitement surrounding the grand jury investigations and the *Oregonian* exposé, Sheriff Schrunk made a point of being at the right place at the right time. Attorney General Robert Thornton later charged that "Schrunk was injecting himself into the thing . . . by issuing statements [and] making political use" of the vice investigation.[71]

The grand jury's indictments of municipal officials were the culmination of decades of vice crime and political corruption in the Rose City, and the case here was similar to cases in several American cities. By the end of 1956, the *Oregonian* headlines attracted national attention, as similar cases had unfolded in Detroit, Chicago, and New York City. The U.S. Senate and FBI investigators were very interested not only in the local crime problem in Portland and allegations of labor racketeering, but also in the city's 1956 mayoral election between Schrunk and Peterson. Throughout the summer of 1956, newspapermen photographed Sheriff Schrunk and his deputies serving warrants on Portland's indicted law enforcement officers and detaining the city's top underworld racketeers. The sheriff created the appearance that he was a tough-on-crime candidate for mayor, when in fact Schrunk cooperated with the Teamsters' attempt to take control of Portland's criminal underground and allegedly took bribes himself from vice racketeers.

The Portland vice scandal implicated top law enforcement officials in the city and clearly showed that previous efforts at reform were ineffective. Now that the general public, and the entire nation for that matter, was fully aware of these criminal activities and their unwelcome implications, it seemed likely another attempt at reform would ensue. Or, would it be business as usual? James Elkins, however, must have known that he committed professional suicide divulging not only the conspiracy, but more important, exposing his own criminal operations, which were immediately shut down.

FIVE

THE McCLELLAN
COMMITTEE

AUGUST 1956 SAW PORTLAND'S TOP LAW ENFORCEMENT OFFI-
cers indicted on a host of corruption charges, which bled into the
upcoming mayoral contest between Sheriff Terry Schrunk and
incumbent Fred Peterson. Schrunk himself was implicated in the
vice scandal that the *Oregonian* had blown wide open and the
accusations were flying. Although urban renewal, transportation,
public housing, and a new civic center topped the list of general
campaign issues, Mayor Fred Peterson instead responded to the
reports of his "unholy alliance" with vice racketeers, the indictments against Police Chief James Purcell, and the apparent oppor-
tunism demonstrated by Sheriff Schrunk during the vice scandal.
At a press conference held at city hall on November 1, 1956, just
days before the election, Chief Purcell read a twelve-page indictment against Sheriff Schrunk that accused him of laxity in law
enforcement and of staging vice raids in the city that the chief
characterized as "token and phony," calculated to embarrass the
mayor and the Portland Police Bureau. Perhaps most embarrassing
was that Portland police officers witnessed the sheriff take a bribe
outside a north Portland club.[1]

Local investigations continued but were brought up short in 1957 when Robert F. Kennedy, chief counsel for the U.S. Senate Subcommittee on Investigations, got involved. This moved Portland to the center stage in the national investigations into urban vice and labor racketeering. By the end of 1956, Kennedy had contacted *Oregonian* reporter Wallace Turner seeking information about the Portland story. In December, Kennedy and Chief Assistant Counsel Jerome Alderman flew to Portland to collect data on allegations that certain Teamsters union officials, especially Western Conference President Frank Brewster and organizer Clyde Crosby, had business relationships with local vice racketeers.

The U.S. Senate Select Committee on Improper Activity in the Labor or Management Field, also known as the McClellan Committee, was created on January 30, 1957, and ended in 1960. The committee was charged with investigating racketeering in labor and management relations, and ended with its focus on corruption within the Teamsters union. While the committee was not the first government attempt to investigate labor unions, the revelations and conclusions of the McClellan Committee had a tremendous impact on the public's perception of labor unions. In fact, many Americans continue to associate the Teamsters with Jimmy Hoffa, Dave Beck, and labor racketeering.

The federal investigation of the Teamsters is best understood in the broader context of Congress's political interest in organized labor, involving pro- or anti-union blocs. Throughout the twentieth century, conservative members of Congress tried desperately to control, and in many cases discredit, labor unions, especially after New Dealers passed the Wagner Act in 1936, which guaranteed workers' rights to organize and bargain collectively. Congressman Clare Hoffman (R-Michigan), a vocal critic of labor unions—especially the Teamsters union—was the first congressman to attack the violent union organizational tactics, powerful union bosses, and the relationship between labor and organized crime. In 1943, Hoffman began his assault by publicizing a conflict between the Detroit Teamsters and the milk drivers in Port Huron, Michigan. The milk drivers refused to join the Teamsters union and, consequently, were threatened with violence. Using a tactic that was successful in the 1937 Brewery Workers Union dispute in Portland, as it had been in many disputes across the country, the Teamsters set up a secondary boycott and threatened to halt all deliveries to grocers, drugstores, and restaurants that accepted non-Teamsters milk.[2] The Teamsters frequently and effectively deployed this organizational tactic to extend unionism into retail, food, and warehouse trades. Although the Democrats at the time controlled the House, Congressman Hoffman's effort helped to ensure the passage of the Hobbs Bill in 1946, which criminalized labor extortion and violence, thereby expanding the scope of criminal racketeering statutes. Later, in 1949, Congressman Hoffman launched an investigation into the use of Teamsters' "goon squads" as an organizational weapon in Kalamazoo, Michigan.[3]

By the summer of 1945, unions represented 35 percent of the civilian workforce and organized labor represented the single largest organized voting bloc in the Democratic Party. In peacetime, labor expected to share in corporate and government labor policy making. President Truman tried to broker an agreement between corporate and labor leaders at a November conference in Washington, D.C., but too many conflicts between the leaders and within the labor faction itself prohibited any agreement on postwar labor policy. Labor strife prevailed. While the conference was taking place, 200,000 United Auto Workers walked out of General Motors plants. In January 1946, 300,000 meat packers and 180,000 electrical workers went on strike; 750,000 steelworkers followed shortly thereafter. It took a federal court injunction against the United Mine Workers and a subsequent contempt charge against its president, John L. Lewis, to force the miners back to work. Within one year after the war, 4,630 strikes involved five million American workers.[4]

At the same time, a coalition of concerned southern Democrats and Republicans were writing anti-labor legislation. Within six weeks of the beginning of the 1947 congressional session, both the House and Senate introduced similar bills to revise the Wagner Act. Congressman Fred Hartley (R-New Jersey) and Senator Robert Taft (R-Ohio) proposed two separate bills designed to "protect the public interests against the actions of power-drunk labor bosses." After a debate in a joint conference committee in 1947, the Taft-Hartley Act was passed, granting business leaders additional rights, while rendering many union practices illegal. The act banned closed shops in which workers had to be union members, reaffirmed the federal courts' power to issue injunctions against strikes and other union tactics, and gave the president the power, in the interest of national security, to seize any struck industry.[5]

Conservative congressmen also attacked alleged Communist-led unions. Historian Nelson Lichtenstein maintains that the "most overtly ideological, best-remembered consequence [of the Taft-Hartley Act] was the purge of the Communists from official union posts." The law required union members to sign an affidavit asserting they were not Communists either ideologically or by organizational affiliation. Only trade unionists were required to sign such an affidavit, not employers, which, Lichtenstein argues, "inscribed in the law a class distinction and a stigma that even the most anti-Communist trade union officials found repugnant." The rival labor federations—the American Federation of Labor and the newer Congress of Industrial Organizations—both contemplated a boycott of the Taft-Hartley Act, but such a protest would deprive their member unions access to the National Labor Relations Board and whatever protection labor laws still provided them. Communists were therefore "sacrificed" to the Cold War's ideological struggle.[6]

At the same time the Taft-Hartley Act was being pushed through Congress, the House Committee on Un-American Activities (HUAC) stepped up its "inquisition" of Communists. Although Communists in the Hollywood film industry and in government departments were the primary targets of HUAC and Senator Joseph McCarthy's (R-Wisconsin) Permanent Subcommittee on Investigations, labor was not exempt. In 1936, FBI Director J. Edgar Hoover, by broadly interpreting an oral directive from President Roosevelt, launched an intensive investigation of alleged Communist influence in maritime, steel, coal, newspaper, and other industries. According to the National Security Electronic Surveillance Card File, the FBI bugged or wiretapped the CIO Council, CIO Maritime Committee, International Longshoremen's and Warehousemen's Union, UAW, UMW, and other left-wing unions. Historians Athan G. Theoharis and John S. Cox explain that Hoover justified the FBI's surveillance of Communist- or radical-led unions as "essential to establishing whether they were subject to Soviet control."[7]

Hoover was also concerned about the unwillingness of Presidents Roosevelt and Truman to take action on his reports of Communists in labor unions and government positions. Therefore, the director leaked information to various public officials, departments, and congressional committees.[8] According to an internal memo, the FBI furnished information on labor union activities to HUAC, Senate Committee on Labor and Public Welfare, Senate Subcommittee on Labor Management Relations, Senate Permanent Subcommittee on Investigations (chaired by Senator McCarthy), and other congressional committees that could influence labor policies and write labor legislation.[9] Historian Ellen Schrecker asserts that FBI agents and HUAC staff members treated alleged Communist-led unions with "enormous hostility" and their leaders as "adjuncts of the Soviet secret police."[10] The solution, according to Hoover, was exposure, and this "line of reasoning," Schrecker argues, was attractive to Congress, vindicated HUAC, and shaped McCarthy-era legislation. The highly publicized McCarthy hearings led Congress to pass the Internal Security Act, or McCarran Act of 1950, which required Communist, Communist-front, and Communist-action organizations to register with the Subversive Activities Control Board. The Communist Control Act of 1954 extended registration to Communist-infiltrated organizations and unions.[11]

Ironically, Teamsters union officials were the kind of business unionists that the architects of Taft-Hartley and anti-Communist legislation wanted to encourage. They were essentially detached from the greater labor movement and were non-ideological. Teamsters' leaders Dave Beck, Frank Brewster, and Jimmy Hoffa were, as Nelson Lichtenstein describes, "nepotistic barons" who saw themselves as "salesmen of labor." The International Brotherhood of Teamsters, however, was bureaucratically and hierarchically decentralized and feudal. Teamsters' locals were militant in the postwar era, self-confident, and aggressive, and in part fragmented, which meant that few companies could withstand a long strike or slowdown. The federal government was particularly interested in the Teamsters because the union could be very disruptive.[12]

In 1950, a highly publicized congressional inquiry into police corruption began, called the Special Committee on Organized Crime in Interstate Commerce—or the Kefauver Committee, named for committee chairman Senator Estes Kefauver (D-Tennessee). The committee also raised questions about organized crime. Hearings began in May and involved testimonies of more than six hundred witnesses in fourteen cities. In New York, over fifty witnesses described the criminal, political, social, and legal activities of the nation's largest crime syndicate, led by Frank Costello. This syndicate, created by Lucky Luciano in the 1930s, was comprised of bootleggers, gamblers, and hit men and developed close relations with Teamsters union officials and business managers and politicians. Allegations of municipal corruption led all the way to the top and eventually forced Mayor William O'Dwyer to resign. While Portland Mayor Dorothy McCullough Lee (1948–1952) was pursuing her ill-fated reform efforts, in Tampa, Florida, the Kefauver Committee exposed a conspiracy involving the sheriff of Hillsborough County who received payments for protecting gamblers; Senate investigators located a "bagman" who carried payoffs of $3,000 to $4,000 per month to each of the thirty-eight police districts in Philadelphia; and in Dade County, Florida, the sheriff's wife served as the "middle-man," transferring payoffs ranging from $7,000 to $11,000 at a time from an organized crime syndicate to her husband

and who, according to Kefauver's investigators, received receipts documenting the transactions.[13] The Kefauver Committee publicized the activities and condemned the sinister influence of organized crime. The committee's exposure of the connection between organized crime and municipal corruption helped to simplify Robert Kennedy's investigation that uncovered the link between organized crime and labor unions.

Congressman George Bender (R-Ohio), as chairman of the Government Operations Subcommittee on Investigations, initiated another investigation into labor unions in 1954, this time an inquiry into bribes Midwestern contractors were forced to pay to the Painters Union of the AFL to compete for jobs.[14] After exposing these payoffs, the so-called Bender Committee then traveled to Cleveland. While the Coin Machine Men of Oregon was organizing the gambling machine industry in Portland in 1954 and 1955, a similar group used Teamsters' muscle to organize the jukebox and vending machine industry in Cleveland. The outcome of this Cleveland investigation highlighted the limits of congressional interest in union corruption. In October 1954, Ohio Teamsters' leaders William Presser and Louis Triscaro were scheduled to testify before the Bender Committee. According to Robert Kennedy, Presser and Triscaro were "Hoffa lieutenants." While the committee was in recess, Presser announced at a meeting of the Ohio Conference of Teamsters that the union supported Congressman George Bender in his candidacy for U.S. Senate. Ohio Teamster Jim Luken later told the McClellan Committee that the Ohio Joint Council of Teamsters solicited contributions from union members for Triscano and Presser's defense fund to defray the $40,000 in expenses they incurred in preparing for the Bender Committee hearings. Luken explained that the legal bills were already paid. Ohio Joint Council President George Starling explained, "Other money was spent to pull certain strings to see that these charges were dropped." The Bender Committee did not reconvene as scheduled in November 1954 and Hoffa later hired George Bender to chair the union's special committee to investigate corruption among the Teamsters. Kennedy later reported that the former congressman was paid over $58,000.[15]

Also in 1954, Congressman Clare Hoffman, now the chairman of the Joint Subcommittee of Government Operations, set out to investigate the Teamsters union again. This time, the congressman looked into allegations that the union was using violent methods to organize industries in Kansas City, Kansas. This congressional investigation then shifted its focus to Detroit in response to rumors that in 1951 Jimmy Hoffa placed an estimated $3 million from the Central States Teamsters' Health and Welfare Fund into the hands of Union Casualty Life Insurance Agency in Chicago. Allen Dorfman, who the subcommittee eventually linked to the Italian crime syndicate in Chicago and the Jewish mob in New York, owned Union Casualty. The subcommittee, moreover, found evidence that Dorfman had invested the Teamsters' fund in illegal operations.[16]

The McClellan Committee originated in the aftermath of the 1954 congressional election when Democrats won control of the U.S. Senate and Senator John McClellan, an Arkansas Democrat, became chairman of the Government Operations Committee, which was the parent of the Senate Subcommittee on Investigations. McClellan exploited the subcommittee's jurisdiction over inefficiency, waste, and malpractice in all departments of the executive branch. Having replaced Republican Senator Joseph McCarthy as head of this subcommittee, Senator McClellan hired Robert Kennedy as the subcommittee's chief counsel and turned the focus away from the alleged subversive activities of Communists and toward allegations of corruption in certain institutions. By 1956, the subcommittee was investigating corruption in the Foreign Operations Administration, an investigation that ultimately revealed that Secretary of the Air Force Harold Talbott profited from contracts awarded to his own engineering firm in New York.[17]

The subcommittee's investigation of union racketeering was rooted in concerns that organized crime influenced some labor unions. At the start of 1956, Robert Kennedy later admitted, he had only a "vague impression" of the corrupt activities of the Teamsters union and officials such as Dave Beck and Jimmy Hoffa. Rather, the investigation was originally triggered by reports of union corruption and rumors that organized crime figures were taking up various leadership positions in union locals throughout the country.

The violent attack on labor columnist Victor Riesel on April 15, 1956, also proved a motivating factor.[18] A few days before the explosive *Oregonian* exposé hit newsstands and linked labor racketeering and organized crime in Portland, Riesel was attacked outside Lindy's restaurant on Broadway in New York City. The perpetrator, Abraham Telvi, threw sulfuric acid in Riesel's face. The columnist had recently reported on corruption in the International Union of Operating Engineers and provided the Justice Department evidence of violence and organized crime in the trucking and garment industry. President Eisenhower reportedly watched Riesel on the television news program *Meet the Press* after the attack and vowed to have the Justice Department investigate the relationship between labor and organized crime. In the ensuing investigation, the FBI linked Telvi to New York labor racketeer Johnny "Dio" Dioguardi, a former soldier for Murder, Incorporated—a group of mafia hit men—and the strongman behind the Teamsters' takeover of the New York trucking industry.[19] Dio formerly worked for famed mobster and Murder, Incorporated boss Albert Anastasia and developed close ties with Teamsters Vice President Jimmy Hoffa.[20]

The subcommittee found that Dio and other racketeers, notably Anastasia, had "muscled" into the New York labor movement. They also uncovered evidence that implicated Hoffa and Dio in a clever scheme to create "paper locals" in New York City. The membership rolls of these fictitious union locals were comprised mostly of small business employees who had been forced to join the union after Dio threatened their employers with possible strikes and extortion. Hoffa controlled these locals, which represented him in the New York Joint Council. This was part of Hoffa's scheme to put him in a position to make a run for president of the International Brother-hood of Teamsters and unseat Dave Beck. The "paper locals," Rob-ert Kennedy explained, wrote checks to fictitious people, forged endorsements, pocketed Teamsters union money, and produced fake membership rolls to create the illusion that loyal Teamsters backed Hoffa and his partners.[21]

Nevertheless, as late as August 1956, Kennedy was still not con-vinced that the committee should investigate the criminal activities of union officials and members. Earlier congressional investigations found little evidence of union racketeering. Moreover, as Kennedy later explained, "there was a question [as to] whether our committee had jurisdiction to conduct such an inquiry." However, Clark Mol-lenhoff, a correspondent for Cowles Publications and considered "the nation's best-informed reporter in the field of labor-management corruption," was convinced that McClellan's Government Opera-tions Committee could in fact claim jurisdiction insofar as unions were tax-exempt organizations and union racketeers in the Mid-west and elsewhere were misusing union funds. The reporter told Kennedy that Jimmy Hoffa admitted in 1953 to having destroyed Teamsters union financial records each year—a crime that violated the Taft-Hartley Act. Based on this information, Senator McClel-lan authorized Kennedy to send investigators to the Midwest and up the East Coast to investigate allegations of union corruption. Later, in November 1956, after consulting the lawyers and counsels from the previous congressional investigations, as well as many of the nation's top newspapermen, Kennedy and financial investigator Carmine Bellino expanded the investigation to the West Coast, par-ticularly Los Angeles, Seattle, and Portland. Kennedy's new initia-tive was motivated by a confidential tip from friend and Teamsters' lawyer Eddie Cheyfitz that West Coast Teamsters' leader Frank Brewster "was the corrupt union figure" he should investigate.[22]

In particular, Kennedy and Bellino investigated the allegations of collusion between the garbage haulers union and an employer association in Los Angeles. As Kennedy later explained, he and

Bellino were particularly intrigued by the 1949 conflict between the Retail Clerks union and the Teamsters that had purportedly involved Midwest gangster "goons."[23] During their late 1956 visit to California, Los Angeles Police Department Captain James Hamilton urged Kennedy and Bellino to travel to Portland to investigate the recent *Oregonian* reports of political corruption, organized crime, and union racketeering. At this time, however, Kennedy only scheduled a trip to Seattle.[24]

While Frank Brewster managed to avoid Kennedy and Bellino during their visit to Seattle, Kennedy remained determined to make some headway in this investigation. *Seattle Times* reporter Ed Guthman, who was conducting his own investigation of the Western Conference of Teamsters, introduced Kennedy, his personal friend, to a group of concerned Teamsters in Local 174, the local founded by Dave Beck and, at that time, controlled by Brewster. These Teamsters provided Kennedy with invoices indicating that Brewster used union funds for his own personal affairs, and that this included money for the maintenance of his thoroughbred horses and stables.[25] On December 15, 1956, Kennedy and Bellino finally caught up with Brewster in Seattle and questioned him about using union funds to finance his race horses and other personal expenses. According to Clark Mollenhoff, Brewster "flew into a rage" and questioned the investigators' veracity. "I might be impressed," Kennedy shot back, "if we didn't already have proof you've lied to us about several things."[26] Even so, Kennedy at the time concluded that Brewster was not necessarily corrupt, but had simply "inherited some of the bad habits of Dave Beck."[27]

Portland was next. By the end of the month, Kennedy and Assistant Counsel Jerome Alderman flew to Portland to meet *Oregonian* reporters Wallace Turner and William Lambert and to collect evidence against Brewster and local Teamsters' official Clyde Crosby. During their brief stay at the Heathman Hotel, Kennedy and his investigators studied Turner's and Lambert's articles as well as Crosby's personal and professional background and his extra-union activities as a Teamsters official. They also investigated Crosby's connection to vice racketeers James Elkins, Thomas Maloney, and Joseph McLaughlin. The investigators looked into the union's participation in Portland's vice rackets and the Seattle group's plan to take over the city's criminal enterprises. Kennedy also investigated the Teamsters' role in District Attorney William Langley's election campaign in 1954. At this point, having acquired a clear picture of Portland's vice scandal, Kennedy and his investigators headed back to Washington, D.C. They were convinced that the Portland case was crucial to their larger investigation involving New York, Detroit, and Chicago.[28]

The evidence of corruption in New York, Detroit, and Chicago was overwhelming. They had discovered the creation of the New York "paper locals" and evidence that known organized crime figures were included in the local Teamsters union membership. Most significantly, the Senate investigators learned that Joe Parisi of Murder, Incorporated was secretary-treasurer of New York's Local 27.[29] In Detroit, Kennedy's men found further evidence that International Brotherhood of Teamsters Vice President Jimmy Hoffa and Local 985 President William Buffalino were guilty of criminal racketeering, extortion, and "gangsterism."[30] In Chicago, where the focus was on Teamsters union President Dave Beck, Kennedy's men interviewed Nathan Shefferman, the labor relations director of Sears, Roebuck and Co. and who was also reportedly Beck's personal shopper. According to an informant Kennedy later identified as "Mr. X," Shefferman, who was the liaison between Sears management and union leaders, used Teamsters' funds to purchase goods, such as automobiles, for Beck.[31] Evidence of violence against the Retail Clerks union was found in Los Angeles, financial records indicated the misdeeds of Brewster and Beck in Seattle, and vice racketeer James Elkins was willing to testify about his business relationship with Northwest Teamsters in Portland.

Kennedy and Senator McClellan were nearly ready to present their case of Teamsters union corruption and racketeering to the public. Yet, the Senate Subcommittee on Investigation continued to struggle to identify its jurisdiction in the matter and to justify its investigation of union racketeering. This subcommittee's jurisdiction was limited to government operations; labor relations were the province of the Senate Labor Committee. By January 1957, however, McClellan and Kennedy discovered this important link: the Teamsters union filed inaccurate and false reports with the secretary of labor, making this a case of "government operations." The federal government "was not functioning efficiently," Kennedy reasoned, "if thousands of reports, filed each year, were never looked at—much less examined."[32] It turns out that the Senate Subcommittee on Investigation had jurisdiction over this apparent mismanagement of an executive department.

On January 30, 1957, the U.S. Senate voted unanimously to create and empower a special select committee—created for special investigations that continued indefinitely—to conduct hearings into racketeering in labor and management relations. To justify the creation of this powerful new committee, Senator McClellan asserted that the six-month investigation conducted by the Government Operations Committee uncovered evidence of fraud in many city governments and that the confirmed breakdown in local government policing indicated that the federal government should take a more aggressive role in combating municipal corruption.[33]

The members of the resulting Senate Select Committee on Improper Activities in the Labor or Management Field—the McClellan Committee—included Democrats John F. Kennedy and Pat McNamara as well as Republicans Barry Goldwater and Irving Ives. All were members of the Senate Labor Committee. Republican Senators Joseph McCarthy and Karl Mundt, as well as Democrats Samuel Ervin and Chairman John McClellan, were from the Permanent Subcommittee on Investigations. (Republican Senator Carl Curtis replaced Senator McCarthy when he died in May 1957.) Senator McClellan chaired the committee, while Robert Kennedy served as chief counsel.[34]

As a member of the Senate Labor Committee, Senator Wayne Morse, a pro-labor Democrat from Oregon, was eligible to sit on the McClellan Committee. Wallace Turner later explained that McClellan opposed Morse's inclusion, fearing that Morse, given his record on labor issues, would act as a defense attorney for the Teamsters. Indeed, as a member of the Senate Labor Committee in 1946—at the time a pro-labor Republican—Morse tried everything in a senator's handbook, including a filibuster, to save labor unions from the Taft-Hartley Act.[35]

Realizing that Turner and his partner William Lambert maintained a good relationship with the Oregon senator, Senator McClellan and Robert Kennedy asked the reporters to convince Morse to turn down the seat. On January 31, 1957, the two reporters marched over to the Senate, where they discovered that certain Teamsters union officials had beaten them to the senator's office. While waiting to see Morse, Turner and Lambert managed to examine the office guest list and saw that Clyde Crosby and "a whole delegation of Teamsters" had visited Morse the day before. Nonetheless, Morse assured the reporters that he was too close to the Teamsters and that he would not serve on the select committee.[36]

On February 26, 1957, the McClellan Committee assembled to hear witness testimony and to determine the extent of labor racketeering in the United States. Among the twenty-one witnesses from the Northwest called to testify were District Attorney William Langley; racketeers James Elkins, Joseph McLaughlin, and Thomas Maloney; Mayor Terry Schrunk; Teamster Clyde Crosby; and *Oregonian* reporters Wallace Turner and William Lambert. The committee considered the testimony of Langley, McLaughlin, Maloney, and Elkins—each of whom had pending indictments against them—so important that the local court allowed them to leave Multnomah County jurisdiction to testify.[37]

The first to testify before the McClellan Committee were reporters Turner and Lambert, who recapped their newspaper exposé. The senators were especially curious as to how the reporters uncovered such startling information about Portland's vice scandal, union racketeering, and municipal corruption. Turner surprised the committee when he disclosed that a large portion of their information came from union members. "Members of the union are scared to death to get out of line," Turner testified. "They were afraid that their union cards at least will be taken up and they will be out of employment." Although many Teamsters were threatened by their superiors, the reporter continued, some felt compelled to tell, at least in confidence, about the inappropriate manipulation tactics practiced by union officials.[38]

As Turner further explained the situation in Portland, he disclosed that Elkins—who would also be testifying before the committee—was a principal source for the explosive exposé, calling Elkins's credibility into question. Elkins was in fact subject to more indictments than any other witness before the committee. The Senate panel asked Turner if he thought Elkins was telling the truth. "What possible difference does it make?" Turner replied. "Since his story is corroborated in hundreds of ways by documents and testimony. I am positive that he is telling the truth."[39] Kennedy had Senate investigators check hotel, telephone, and travel records to make sure that Elkins was telling the truth.[40] "His story was checked in every possible way," journalist Clark Mollenhoff reported in *Atlantic Monthly*. "Corroboration was produced by the bushel."[41] The committee itself would conclude in 1958 that, "while the committee in no way excuses Elkins for any activities he may have engaged in the past, . . . the fact remains that most of Elkins's story stands corroborated . . . by independent evidence."[42]

Testifying at length before the committee, Elkins outlined his vice rackets and described in detail his agreements with Teamsters bosses Frank Brewster, Clyde Crosby, and John Sweeney, his association with Seattle racketeers Maloney and McLaughlin, and the arrangements he made with certain officers in the Portland Police Bureau and with District Attorney William Langley. The racketeer also admitted to a partnership with Langley at the China Lantern nightclub and conceded that illegal gambling took place in the back rooms. Despite Langley's insistence that this partnership was dissolved in 1950, the reality was that his relationship with Elkins continued into the early 1950s, and intensified following Langley's election as district attorney in 1954. As district attorney, Langley kept the racketeer informed when warrants were issued for raids or of any planned abatement of a nightclub. Elkins further explained that certain Teamsters officials and vice racketeers met with District Attorney Langley at the Olympic Hotel in Seattle, where they discussed Portland's criminal rackets.[43]

In his testimony, Elkins admitted to bugging Thomas Maloney's Portland King Tower apartment in 1955 and to recording many conversations between Maloney and Langley that he planned to use as blackmail. He explained that he taped a conversation between District Attorney Langley and Oregon Liquor Control Commissioner Thomas Sheridan, who at the time was being investigated by a Multnomah County grand jury for accepting bribes from illegal liquor operations that Langley made little effort to curb. Although Langley continued to deny the allegations, the King Tower tapes revealed that the district attorney was part of a grand jury whitewash to present the illusion that something was being done about the after-hours clubs.[44]

The McClellan Committee listened to the King Tower tapes and, despite many reports that most of the recordings were indecipherable, concluded that District Attorney Langley "was a definite participant in the plot to open up vice and gambling in Portland."[45] On the tapes, District Attorney Langley complained about his "piddling" share of the $20,000 that Elkins had paid the group as their share from the Portland rackets. Langley was heard counting the payoffs and repeatedly emphasized his desire to frame Elkins.[46] "Had we not had those tapes," Wallace Turner recalled in 2002, "we could not have proved what [information Elkins] had." Turner remembered, "I heard him [Langley] counting out the money that [Maloney] had handed him, and demanding to know from which illegal gambling source it came . . . [and] making plans to put Elkins in jail."[47]

Appearing before the McClellan Committee on March 14, 1957, and accompanied by his lawyer whom he consulted after each question, William Langley "hardly looked the part, nor did his wife, who accompanied him," recalled Robert Kennedy. "He seemed more like a man on his way to his twentieth reunion at an Ivy League college, than a discredited district attorney on his way to the Senate caucus room to take the Fifth Amendment."[48] The district attorney declined to answer any questions on the grounds that his answers might incriminate him during his forthcoming trial in Portland. Rather than denying the allegations, Langley invoked his Fifth Amendment rights when he was asked if he ever received or transferred money that was earned by criminal rackets and when he was questioned about his association with Elkins, Crosby, Maloney, McLaughlin, Sweeney, or Brewster.[49]

Kennedy was particularly interested in whether or not Teamsters union officials profited from vice income or used union dues to finance vice operations. When Kennedy later questioned Thomas Maloney about his vice income, his receipt of Teamsters' loans, and his relationship with Frank Brewster, the racketeer refused to answer, invoking his right not to provide answers that could be used to strengthen the case against him back in Portland.[50] Represented by former Portland City Prosecutor Charles Raymond, Joseph McLaughlin also declined to comment on any of the information Elkins provided the committee. McLaughlin's silence, in effect, robbed the committee of any evidence that could potentially be used against the corrupt Teamsters leaders.[51]

Unlike Langley, Maloney, and McLaughlin, who exercised their Fifth Amendment rights, Clyde Crosby publicly denied the accusations that he was involved with the Seattle group and delivered a defense. Although there was plenty of evidence offered in news reports and sworn testimony that Elkins was a vice racketeer, Crosby, with Mayor Terry Schrunk, nonetheless, gave the McClellan Committee "unsworn and unsigned" statements from two Portland prostitutes that Elkins was a pimp and a narcotics trafficker, an attempt to discredit the committee's star witness. The women later recanted during interviews with the committee, claiming that they embellished the stories because they feared Schrunk and Crosby. According to the McClellan Committee, the pair threatened to send the two prostitutes to Oregon's insane asylum if they did not support their defense.[52]

Elkins's testimony also exposed newly elected Portland Mayor Terry Schrunk. Schrunk was alleged to have taken a bribe in 1955 outside of north Portland's 8212 Club, operated by Clifford "Slim" Bennett and owned by Elkins himself. Elkins paid Joseph McLaughlin and Thomas Maloney a percentage of the club's profits, but when the Seattle racketeers became unhappy with the disappointing size of their payout, they contacted Raymond Kell, a Portland lawyer and friend of Schrunk. As Elkins told the committee, McLaughlin and Maloney told Kell that Schrunk should raid and close the club, thus sending Elkins a message that the Seattle group was dissatisfied with the present arrangement. Schrunk discussed the situation with Kell and then allegedly warned Bennett that he would arrest everyone exiting the club unless he was paid a bribe.[53]

According to Elkins, eyewitnesses, and state investigators, in the early morning hours of September 11, 1955, two Multnomah County sheriff deputies entered the 8212 Club while illegal drinks were being served and gambling "was in full swing." After he intercepted the two deputies, club manager Clifford Bennett went downstairs and outside with one of the deputies and spoke to Sheriff Schrunk. When Bennett returned to the club, witnesses heard him explaining that Schrunk was unhappy because Bennett "had taken care of everybody else, but he had forgotten to take care of him [Schrunk]." Bennett picked up the telephone and attempted to call Elkins but was unsuccessful. Bennett then asked Elkins henchman, John Vance, if "it was better to pay out $500 tonight rather than

$1,500 the next day?" Vance told Bennett that he thought payment that night was "a pretty smart thing to do."[54] Bennett then put $500 in a manila envelope, walked out of the club and across the street and dropped the envelope behind a utility pole. Several witnesses, including three Portland police officers, saw Schrunk walk over and pick up the envelope. Shocked by what he just witnessed, Portland Police Officer Dick Sutter exclaimed, "That crooked son-of-a-bitch." After making the exchange with Schrunk, Bennett confidently invited more guests into the club: "Come on in and have a drink. Everything is O.K."[55]

The next day, Bennett was supposed to return the nightly bankroll of $1,500 to Elkins's accountant, Laura Stone, but was $500 short. "I asked him where the other $500 was," Stone testified, "and [Bennett] said he used it to take care of someone." Stone later told the McClellan Committee that she had never heard that expression before, so she asked Bennett what he meant. Bennett then told her that he "gave it to Terry Schrunk."[56] When Elkins later confronted Bennett about the missing $500, Bennett told him that he thought it was better "to give [Schrunk] that than to pay $1,500 or $2,000 for having the place pinched."[57]

State and federal documents, eyewitness reports, and the King Tower tapes show that when Schrunk was sheriff he had agreements with vice racketeers James Elkins, Clifford Bennett, Al Winter, and Stanley Terry, allowing vice properties to operate unmolested. Many who were close to Schrunk did not believe the charges and were convinced that he was being framed.[58] But a deputy sheriff working under Sheriff Schrunk told the Oregon State Police in 1956 that a clerk in the county criminal department was the "payoff man for the sheriff" and had been for many years.[59]

While Schrunk did not oppose certain vice operations, if the operators abused the favor, he would be quick to shut them down. The King Tower tapes are illuminating in this regard, as the following excerpt shows. Here District Attorney Langley, Thomas Maloney, and Joseph McLaughlin are discussing their relationship with

James Elkins and deliberating whether to open gambling operations in the county:

> LANGLEY: The only thing that'd happen there [in the county] is that [Stanley] Terry'd scream like hell.
>
> MCLAUGHLIN: Oh, I don't think he'd [Terry] care.
>
> MALONEY: He's the only one that can go into Schrunk?
>
> LANGLEY: Well, you guys got—gotta change your tactics. You either get rid of the mayor and that finishes the Character [Elkins] or you go into the county.
>
> MCLAUGHLIN: You say Terry's the only one who can talk to Schrunk?
>
> MALONEY: That's right. He's the only one that can go direct into him and hand him some money. That I know for a positive fact. . . . Now, I went into Schrunk cold turkey about that thing—about that out in the county thing. Like places Al Winters and them guys has. And . . . here's the answer he give me, he says, "Tom, the reason why I don't want to give you an okeh on it, I just want to help a friend of mine." He says, "Tom, I closed it, because Mr. Al Winters and Sonny Heath thought they were too big for me." . . . That Schrunk is the one that went out there and raised hell and closed (indistinct) because they didn't tell him—they didn't tell him to see 'em.
>
> LANGLEY: It looks to me like either you knock the—this Purcell out of the box or else you try to go into the county and use your connections with Schrunk.[60]

In the fall of 1956, Thornton presented further evidence to the state grand jury that Schrunk accepted bribes in exchange for ignoring certain vice properties.[61] The grand jury subpoenaed Schrunk to testify about his version of the 8212 Club incident, and Schrunk also submitted to the jury's request for a lie-detector test.[62] The test, though not definitive, suggested that the sheriff was not telling the truth when asked about the 8212 Club incident, particularly when he denied that he received a package that night from club manager Clifford Bennett. A senior Oregon State Police investigator noted in his report that he personally believed that Schrunk accepted the bribe from Clifford Bennett.[63] The grand jury, nonetheless, determined that the evidence was still insufficient for an indictment.

According to some reports, it is likely that without the pressure of local Teamsters union officials on Multnomah County commissioners, Schrunk might not have been appointed to the sheriff's post in 1948 to begin with.[64] Schrunk's relationship with union officials, racketeer Thomas Maloney, and mob boss Joseph McLaughlin subsequently blossomed during the 1954 district attorney election when, as sheriff, he ordered the removal of a sound truck promoting William Langley from a livestock show at the exposition center. James Elkins told the McClellan Committee that he and the Teamsters paid for the truck. Maloney called Teamsters official John Sweeney in Seattle and Sweeney then contacted Schrunk in Portland. The next day, the truck returned to the show along with additional campaign material to re-elect Schrunk as sheriff.[65]

In February 1956, Terry Schrunk announced his candidacy for Portland mayor with the promise, according to former Schrunk aid Mary Tobkin, that he would create employment opportunities and run a "good, clean, decent police department."[66] It is possible that Schrunk's decision to run for mayor was the reason that James Elkins approached the *Oregonian* with his recordings; moreover, Schrunk's candidacy may have encouraged the pro-Republican newspaper to print the exposé implicating Teamsters officials and the pro-labor Democrat Sheriff Schrunk. As a tool of the Oregon Republican party, which now faced a serious challenge from the Democratic party, the *Oregonian*, Joseph Uris argues, had an interest in curbing Democratic success, and arrangements between racketeers and the city's law enforcement officials depended upon the "maintenance of the predominantly Republican city administration led . . . by Fred Peterson."[67]

Portlanders first heard of Terry Schrunk's relationship with the vice racketeers when Mayor Fred Peterson and Police Chief Jim Purcell read the new indictments on November 1, 1956. Subsequently, at his own news conference on November 3, Schrunk condemned the "kamikaze" actions of Peterson and Purcell, undertaken just days before the mayoral election, and declared his hopes that the public had perceived the stunt as a political maneuver. One week later, the sheriff triumphed in the mayoral elections, thereby proving, or so it seemed, that the charges against him were groundless. The outgoing mayor's defeat was decisive. After sixteen years of public service, Fred Peterson was defeated by a margin of more than 38,000 votes.[68]

Mayor Terry Schrunk joined the other twenty McClellan Committee witnesses from the Pacific Northwest. In his testimony, he denied having received a bribe outside the 8212 Club. When asked about the polygraph he took during the Oregon State grand jury investigation in 1956, Schrunk admitted that he failed the test.[69] According to Wallace Turner, Senator Karl Mundt "baited Schrunk" and convinced him to take another test to support his testimony that he never accepted payoffs while sheriff. The Secret Service administered this polygraph, but Schrunk walked out midway through the questioning. Turner later said that Schrunk was prepared only to answer questions about his drinking problem or about the alleged envelope swap outside the 8212 Club, which according to Sidney Lezak, former U.S. attorney for Oregon, were directly related. He refused to answer questions about his relationship with James Elkins and other vice racketeers.[70]

Schrunk accused the Senate staff of asking "loaded" questions and then criticized the integrity and capability of the Secret Service.[71] According to the McClellan Committee's *Interim Report*, Schrunk refused to answer the following six questions:

1. Are you personally acquainted with Jim Elkins?
2. While in a restaurant, did you receive several hundred dollars that was sent by Jim Elkins?
3. While sheriff, did you receive any payoffs from Stan Terry?

4. While sheriff, did you receive any payoffs from any pinball operators?
5. While sheriff, did you receive any payoffs from bootleggers through [friend and lawyer] Ray Kell?
6. While sheriff, did you receive any payoffs from any gamblers?[72]

Schrunk protested that these questions were not relevant to the committee's inquiry into labor racketeering. The committee justified its line of questioning by citing evidence that Elkins paid off Schrunk with money from a club that also financed McLaughlin and Maloney, two organized crime figures with deep connections to the Western Conference of Teamsters.[73]

In his defense, Schrunk presented an affidavit signed by Portland Police Officer Dick Sutter, who testified earlier that he witnessed Schrunk receive the bribe outside the 8212 Club in September 1955. Refuting his own earlier Oregon State grand jury testimony, Sutter denied having witnessed any graft:

I observed the fellow who did run the place, whom I believe to be Slim Bennett, walk across the street. And, I certainly don't remember him walking diagonally as the other account states in the paper, because I think I would have pinched him for jay-walking. But, anyway, I observed this Bennett by this telephone pole and this drinking fountain. And, as I recall, he—at least it appeared that he bent down and placed something between the pole and the drinking fountain. And then we observed another man whom at the time I believed to be Sheriff Schrunk go over, and it seemed that he picked something up there. And, what it was that this person picked up, I can't say. But I told the grand jury in my testimony that it was Sheriff Schrunk, but since I have thought a lot about the thing and I have since been convinced— and I will repeat that—have since been convinced it wasn't the sheriff at all, and I am not even sure whoever it was picked anything up there. And, that is the reason that I contacted Mr.

[Officer] Minielly and wanted to talk to the sheriff was that I wanted to straighten it up in that the newspaper account accuses the sheriff of picking it up and apparently it comes from something I have said.[74]

Other affidavits countered Sutter's testimony. Portland Police Officers Merlin Tiedeman and Lowell Amundson quoted Sutter's own reference to Schrunk as a "crooked son-of-a-bitch," a remark Sutter made upon seeing the sheriff take the bribe outside the 8212 Club. Portland Police Officer Kenneth Lindholm's affidavit claimed that Sutter returned to his police car that night and told him that he saw the sheriff pick up the package.[75]

The Senate panel and Kennedy poked more holes in Schrunk's defense by calling Sutter's current partner, Bobby McClendon, to testify against him. McClendon explained that Sutter told him and the state grand jury, in great detail, that Terry Schrunk was "a crooked man." McClendon added that Sutter also admitted that he accepted payoffs to overlook certain vice operations. McClendon further added that after Officer Sutter was subpoenaed by the state grand jury in February 1957, Sutter approached McClendon and tried to convince him not to tell the grand jury the details of their conversations. Officer McClendon told the Senate Committee:

I could not lie to the grand jury and I would not take a chance of being indicted for perjury. Sutter then claimed he wasn't asking me to lie and stated that if I were asked about these conversations with him I should be vague and evasive and that I should tell the grand jury that I could not remember the conversations. I told Sutter that I would not know what it was all about until I got in the grand jury room.[76]

McClendon's testimony hurt Sutter's as well as Schrunk's credibility. Chief Counsel Kennedy continued to press Schrunk, further weakening his defense. Then, suddenly, the mayor refused to cooperate with the committee, arguing that it lacked jurisdiction in this local vice crime corruption case. "After considering and spending about eleven days around here," the mayor complained, "in my opinion this matter is going to be settled in the courts in the state of Oregon. I shall rest on that."[77]

The McClellan Committee inquiry ended in 1960 after hearing testimony for nearly three years and compiling fifty-seven volumes of transcripts. The committee had little direct legislative impact. The only bill that resulted was the Landrum-Griffin Act of 1959, which tightened Taft-Hartley restrictions against secondary boycotts, authorized the Labor Department to regulate union financial affairs, and created a labor union membership "bill of rights" that included provisions for fairer union elections, freedom of opinion, and the setting of membership dues.[78] But the committee did excel in its purpose of publicizing the extent of labor racketeering and municipal corruption.

Historian James Jacobs argues that the hearings were a significant turning point in labor union reform and inspired further investigations of labor racketeering in the 1960s, '70s, and '80s.[79] The principal consequence of the committee, historian Anthony Baltakis concluded, was the promotion of partisan infighting among Democrats and Republicans in Congress, and the decline of organized labor.[80] Historian Nelson Lichtenstein agreed that the hearings "had a devastating impact on the moral standing of the entire trade-union world, belying labor's claim that it constituted the most important and efficacious movement for democracy and social progress." The much-publicized spectacle "marked a true shift in the public perception of American trade unionism."[81] Historians Ralph C. James and Estelle Dinerstein James describe in devastating detail the serious implications of the McClellan Committee investigations for the Teamsters as a union. The organization's ability to negotiate good-faith contracts with ownership and management would be stalled and the reputations of the hard-working, dues-paying membership were soiled. The adverse publicity and the unfavorable congressional findings were so damning that the leadership of the AFL-CIO expelled the Teamsters from the federation in December 1957.[82]

The most significant impact of the McClellan Committee was the undeniable link it exposed between the Teamsters union, corruption, and organized crime, forever after linked in the public consciousness. Robert Kennedy later admitted that although he did not get his man—Jimmy Hoffa—"the awakening of the public [is] what [is] important."[83] Enough evidence was gathered for the indictment and then conviction, in 1957, of Teamsters union President Dave Beck in Seattle. This conviction, Kennedy later explained, "knocked from a position of power a major political figure who, more than any one man, had dominated the state's affairs."[84] Beck's reputation within the Teamsters suffered greatly; in 1958 members of his own union burned him in effigy.[85]

Meanwhile, in 1957 Frank Brewster, president of the Western Conference of Teamsters, was convicted of contempt of Congress for challenging the authority of the Senate Committee on Government Operations, the forerunner of the McClellan Committee. The U.S. Court of Appeals later overturned this conviction, and despite evidence linking him to organized crime in Seattle and Portland, the Teamster official was never convicted of any criminal offense.[86] Brewster was expelled from the union in May 1960 for "alleged irregularities" in his handling of union funds.

The Portland case was vital to the national investigation. The Portland vice scandal exposed by the *Oregonian* provided the crucial evidence for the committee to link the Teamsters with municipal corruption and organized crime. The hearings opened with testimony from the *Oregonian* reporters, and Kennedy and the committee senators credited the Portland vice scandal with being their strongest case against labor racketeering and a large step toward reform. The hearings, moreover, successfully—unfortunately for some—aired Portland's dirty laundry for the nation to see. Senator Karl Mundt (R-South Dakota) berated District Attorney Langley:

You embarrass yourself . . . and it is very embarrassing to me as a citizen of this country to find any district attorney presently sitting in that office, hiding behind the Fifth Amendment. It is embarrassing to me to think of the people of Portland, Oreg., with a mayor who flunks a lie-detector test and a district attorney hiding behind the Fifth Amendment. If I lived there I would suggest they pull the flags down at half mast in public shame.[87]

EPILOGUE

The Fallout

THE 1957–1960 MCCLELLAN COMMITTEE HEARINGS HAD TRE-
mendous political and social impact on Portland. Top officials were
indicted, law enforcement was branded corrupt all the way from the
police chief and county sheriff through the city's district attorney,
and clear connections to organized crime were laid bare. But the
close of the committee hearings did not bring an end to turmoil in
Portland. Many local citizens rejected the federal McClellan hearings as a witch hunt, though state investigations and prosecutions
had been ongoing ever since the *Oregonian* exposed the vice scandal
in 1956. Additional allegations were made and the two daily newspapers warred over which one was more accurate and forthcoming
about the scandal.

When Mayor Terry Schrunk returned to Portland in March
1957, after having refused to testify further before the McClellan
Committee, he surrendered to state authorities. Following his federal testimony, the mayor's indictment for bribery was amended to
include a charge that in 1956 he lied to a state grand jury when
it was investigating Portland's vice scandal.[1] The trial jury heard
opening arguments in the Schrunk case in June 1957. Prosecutors

called twenty-three witnesses, including James Elkins. The rack-eteer, still under indictment himself, testified that his bankroll for the 8212 Club was short $500 the morning after the alleged payoff to Schrunk. Elkins told the jury, however, that he knew nothing more about Schrunk accepting bribes other than what 8212 Club manager Clifford Bennett had told him.[2] This statement is false according to numerous sources. The *Oregonian* reported that Elkins admitted to nurturing a business relationship with Schrunk in which Elkins supported Schrunk politically in exchange for Schrunk preventing any police action from hindering his vice activities. Elkins later tes-tified, and an Oregon State Police report corroborated, that on one occasion in 1955 he visited the sheriff's department in response to a call from Schrunk requesting that the racketeer contribute money and whiskey to an upcoming law enforcement convention. Deputy Sheriff Elmer Wallen corroborated Elkins's testimony. According to Wallen, Schrunk asked the deputy to help organize the conven-tion finances, and Wallen collected contributions from Elkins and other local racketeers, including Stanley Terry and north Portland racketeer Tom Johnson.[3] Despite strong evidence that he had ties to Elkins, Schrunk presented a strong defense during the subsequent trial. His lawyers built their case around the theory that the mayor was the target of a conspiracy led by James Elkins and the *Orego-nian* newspaper.

During the Schrunk trial, the state prosecutor delivered a sur-prise witness to challenge Schrunk's solid defense. On June 26, much to the astonishment of everyone in the courtroom, Robert Kennedy appeared in the Multnomah County courtroom. The first thing that Kennedy told the court was that both *Oregonian* reporter Wallace Turner and racketeer James Elkins tried to discourage him from investigating Schrunk. "Mr. Turner and Mr. Elkins said at that time," Kennedy testified, "that they thought it would be a mis-take to go into it . . . that we had been going along well as we were and that to get into somebody as big as Mayor Schrunk, they did not think it advisable." Kennedy claimed that he then told Turner and Elkins that he was interested only in the facts and did not care who was involved.[4] "Terry [Schrunk] was not one of the people we were after," Wallace Turner later explained. The primary targets of the *Oregonian* reporters' exposé were the corrupt Teamsters union officials and District Attorney William Langley, who had used their positions for their own personal financial gain. Back in Washington, D.C., however, Kennedy told Turner, "One of us is the Chief Counsel of the Select Committee and one of us is not, and we're going to call Schrunk," meaning that Schrunk would be compelled to testify about his relationship with Portland vice racketeers and corrupt Teamsters officials.[5]

Disgruntled union members praised the Senate's investigation in letters that flooded the nation's capital. "I am happy to see that the United States Government is finally beginning to investigate abuse of power by some of the labor 'unions' that know they are above the law," a union member wrote Senator McClellan.[6] "Our relationship with the Union has come to the point where we are never even given the courtesy of a discussion of Union demand. The contracts are brought to us to sign 'or else,'" a Klamath Falls Teamster wrote.[7] A member of the Heat and Frost Insulators Union wrote in April 1957, "We would like very much to have a cleanup in our union; it is very small but very corrupt, and run with a very highhand [sic]."[8]

Some historians, nevertheless, question the committee's and Chief Counsel Robert Kennedy's motivation for their aggressive and very public attack on the Teamsters and Portland's local officials. "Kennedy pursued his own agenda," historian Anthony Baltakis argues, "directing events ensuring what was perceived as proper coverage of the select committee by the media so as to garner publicity for his brother's political ambition and most likely his own as well."[9] Kennedy used the Portland vice scandal, Wallace Turner later argued, for "its attention-getting value as the curtain raiser for getting into Teamster corruption."[10]

Local Teamsters, political officials, and citizens, angrily criticized the committee's agenda. Portland Teamsters union organizer

Amil Spada opined in 2002 that the union was simply a "scape-goat" and leaders Frank Brewster, Clyde Crosby, and others were "railroaded."[11] Portlanders in particular complained that the committee unfairly targeted their city. "You and your committee," one disgruntled "taxpayer" wrote Senator McClellan, "are giving the citizens of Portland, Oregon a 'blackeye'[sic]."[12] "My wife and I, and our daughter . . . are absolutely furious about the ruthlessness of your destruction of Terry Schrunk. . . . What kind of evil is your senatorial inquisition?" complained another Portlander.[13] Most complaints criticized the committee for accusing Portland law enforcement officials of misconduct "without evidence," in other words, based on the word of convicted felon and racketeer James Elkins.[14]

These attitudes played out in the Schrunk trial. After hearing testimony from about sixty witnesses, jurors took less than two hours to acquit their mayor of all charges in 1957. As jurors gleamed with pride—seemingly saving Portland from total embarrassment—175 spectators in the courtroom applauded the verdict. "We have a future in Portland—and now we can get down to work," Mayor Schrunk told the press in his post-trial statement.[15]

The Portland case continued to affect national politics as well. Local attitudes likely affected results in the 1960 presidential campaign and the 1968 Democratic primary. Most evidence suggests that John Kennedy lost Oregon to Richard Nixon in 1960 because he was from the East Coast, while Nixon was from California, and that Kennedy was Catholic and the majority of Oregonians were Protestants.[16] But in 1961, political scientist John M. Swarthout suggested that Kennedy lost to Nixon in Oregon partly because "organized labor never warmed to Mr. Kennedy."[17] Albert Wesley Barthelmes, Robert Kennedy's press secretary during the mid-1960s, suggested that in 1969 organized labor despised both Kennedys for their positions on the McClellan Committee and lobbied against their elections. Barthelmes later explained that he told Robert Kennedy, "The labor movement in Oregon, which is doubtful enough toward John Kennedy, didn't like you [Robert Kennedy], didn't want you, blamed you for that. . . . And Terry Schrunk—this was another thing." Barthelmes continued:

> The McClellan Committee had told him [Schrunk] to come east and testify on the Teamsters' connections in Portland. Robert Kennedy had really taken Schrunk over the coals. There was a very rough questioning session. The thing that the Senator [then Chief Counsel Robert Kennedy], understandably, had not known was that Terry Schrunk was still mayor of Portland, and is still the mayor of Portland nine, ten years later.[18]

After Robert Kennedy's defeat in Oregon during the 1968 presidential primary election, Kennedy telephoned Wallace Turner: "Wally, what's the matter with those people in Oregon?" Turner replied, "Terry Schrunk, Robert."[19] The McClellan Committee hearings depicted Portland as a seedy, little vice-ridden town that elected a corrupt sheriff to be mayor, and it is possible that pro-labor Oregon Democrats who remembered the hearings took their frustrations out on Kennedy by voting for Eugene McCarthy.

Following his trial and acquittal, Mayor Schrunk quickly distanced himself from his Teamsters supporters. Despite managing to stay in office for four complete terms—from 1957 to 1972—no significant city reform emerged from Mayor Schrunk's office. A few Portlanders outside city hall initiated an effort to reform city government. One plan called for a "council-manager" form of municipal governance, therefore, making the position of mayor have less authority with little legislative power. The City Club of Portland advocated a "strong-mayor" plan, which would actually give the mayor virtually dictatorial power. The city council and mayor were criticized at the time for a lack of initiative and effectiveness, and progressive government reform seemed to be the answer. Ultimately, no changes were made to Portland's model of municipal government.

The media, however, closely scrutinized the mayor and public activism pressured law enforcement officials to close brothels and push gambling and unlicensed bars out of the city. Schrunk's friend and campaign manager, lawyer Ray Kell, told sociologist Joseph Uris in 1980 that the "negative publicity, humiliation and expense of the trial meant a real change in his attitudes and politics. Schrunk, an open easy-going liberal, became a cautious, far more conservative and somewhat disenchanted man." Moreover, Mayor Schrunk became "more suspicious."[20] Unlike the great mayors of the 1950s and 1960s, such as Philadelphia's Joseph S. Clark Jr., or New York's John V. Lindsay, Terry Schrunk was not a reformer. As historian Carl Abbott argues, he staked his career on urban renewal, but ultimately "represented the political consensus of the 1950s."[21]

Between August 1956 and September 1957, three different grand juries in Portland handed down 115 indictments, of which fifty-nine were ultimately dismissed. According to Oregon State Attorney General Robert Thornton, the bulk of the indictments were thrown out because many of the state's witnesses, such as James Elkins, had criminal records or were under indictment or both. Nevertheless, the attorney general later acknowledged that the Portland vice scandal investigation was horribly mismanaged. For example, Thornton violated Oregon law by failing to list the names of all the witnesses who testified in each case, thereby nullifying many of the indictments.[22] Wallace Turner later explained that many of the indictments were thrown out because the attorney general moved a grand jury out of the county courthouse and into a nearby state building when recording devices were discovered in the courthouse jury room.[23] By moving the grand jury out of the courthouse, the attorney general violated another Oregon statute.

Among Thornton's sharpest critics was Arthur Kaplan, one of the attorney general's more capable assistants. In a 1957 open letter to his former boss, Kaplan, who was later hired as an investigator for the McClellan Committee, accused the attorney general of "attempting to whitewash the prosecution for political or personal motives." Kaplan specifically charged that Thornton moved evidence and relevant transcripts of testimony from Portland to Salem without explanation, and failed to make the necessary provisions for paying special prosecutors and assistants during the state's investigation. Kaplan further revealed that Thornton prohibited him and Assistant Attorney General Ralph Wycoff from presenting a legal defense of indictments under "technical attack" when many of the dismissed indictments were later reargued before the grand jury; Thornton only allowed the "minimum amount of evidence . . . instead of allowing for a continued full-scale inquiry to develop new evidence for use at trial."[24]

The most damaging accusation, however, was that Thornton failed to deny or explain charges that he had accepted a bribe as the state's chief law enforcement officer. While conducting an attack on organized prostitution as attorney general in 1952, and in the midst of a re-election campaign, an individual approached Thornton offering to contribute a large amount of money to the Democratic Party—reportedly around $6,000—if Thornton would cease his current assault on the vice industry. Apparently, the attorney general discussed the proposition with his assistant at the time, Howard Lonergan, and the two discussed whether or not they should notify the FBI to pursue the attempted bribery case. Thornton finally decided that the evidence was too thin and remote and that an investigation of bribery would be pointless. Nevertheless, in 1956, Lonergan, since hired by William Langley to be his assistant district attorney, told a Multnomah County grand jury that his former boss, Attorney General Thornton, accepted the payoff in 1952 and then swept the investigation under the rug. In his presentation to the grand jury, Lonergan suggested that it was Portland vice racketeer James Elkins who allegedly bribed the attorney general.[25] Thornton later argued that just as he was taking over the Portland vice investigation, his former assistant Lonergan was attempting to discredit him and distract the grand jury from their task of delivering indictments to those involved in the vice scandal.[26] Despite the allegations and criticism of how he managed the Portland vice scandal, Attorney General Thornton held the position until 1969.

The Portland vice scandal began with sensational stories of backroom gambling, prostitution rings, municipal graft, and corrupt union leadership and ended with the nullification of many indictments and the acquittals of some defendants. Of those whose cases actually went to trial, only William Langley, James Elkins, and Elkins's employee Raymond Clark were convicted, although a brothel madam pleaded guilty and was fined $250. Despite the overwhelming evidence against him, Langley was only convicted of refusing to prosecute gamblers. For this he was fined a petty sum of $428.[27]

The evidence against District Attorney Langley was very strong. The King Tower tapes were very damaging to his credibility; Langley was heard on the recordings discussing his whitewash of the Thomas Sheridan–Oregon Liquor Control Commission bribery case, planning with the Seattle group to take over James Elkins's crime syndicate, and counting money he received from a Chinese gambling operation. Despite the tapes being unintelligible in some spots, Langley's voice "came over better than anyone else's and there is no question [of Langley's complicity]," Attorney General Robert Thornton asserted. "Langley's voice [was] 100 percent authentic. Absolutely [it was] the voice of William Langley on these recordings."[28] In 1980, former *Oregonian* reporter William Lambert insisted that it was definitely Langley talking on the tapes because he had a "very distinctive voice."[29]

Moreover, District Attorney William Langley was paid to investigate and subsequently prosecute criminals. Yet Langley did not act against the widespread control and illegal activities of Elkins until after the racketeer made his own disclosures of corruption and vice. State and local records indicate that District Attorney Langley, former Sheriff Terry Schrunk, and the Portland Police Bureau did not act against Elkins until he made his accusations against the district attorney and the Teamsters in 1956. Thus, the loudest critics of

James Elkins and the information he provided prosecutors and the senate committee were the very people who were in a position, and had the duty, to prosecute him for his dubious activities. The "vice czar" of Portland was arrested for the first time just shortly after the *Oregonian* exposé hit newsstands.

After Mayor Schrunk was acquitted, Portland's vice scandal descended to the back pages of the city's newspapers. The remaining controversy seemed to focus on the alleged roles of the city's dailies in the bribery and vice scandals. The *Oregon Journal* released an editorial in April 1957 that broadly criticized the *Oregonian*'s exposé. The editorial coincided with a three-part series titled "Let's Look at the Facts," which maintained that its rival left many aspects of the vice scandal unexplained. It criticized the *Oregonian* for protecting "from the harsh glare of publicity the full infamous record of its star witness—the hoodlum, thug, narcotics peddler and ex-convict known as 'Big Jim' Elkins." The *Journal* accused *Oregonian* reporters Wallace Turner and William Lambert of deliberately ignoring the corruption in Portland's Police Bureau because any exposure would have embarrassed Elkins and Mayor Fred Peterson, the *Oregonian*'s candidate for mayor.[30] The *Journal* editors set out to prove that the *Oregonian* minimized Elkins's role in the scandal. The *Journal* stated that after a brief sketch of the racketeer's criminal record in an April issue of the *Oregonian*, the *Oregonian* ran twenty-two stories about Elkins on twenty-one different days. Each article, the *Journal* charged, lessened the racketeer's role by describing him as "merely a nightlife bankroller" or a "financier of fringe operations."[31]

The *Oregonian*, nonetheless, captured the nation's attention with stories about the Rose City's brush with organized crime, a phenomenon thought only to exist in the big metropolises of New York, Chicago, Miami, and Los Angeles. Moreover, the *Oregonian* exposé in 1956 was vital, if not central, to the federal investigation into labor racketeering. Meanwhile, the *Journal* watched as its rival won a Pulitzer Prize and received attention from Robert Kennedy, the McClellan Committee, and the national press, such as *Time*, while reporters Turner and Lambert were awarded the Heywood Broun Award for journalistic excellence.

The *Journal* argued that they printed all sides of the story, criticizing the *Oregonian* for their seemingly biased, whitewashed approach to journalism. The *Journal*, for example, allowed the accused to tell their side of the story. District Attorney William Langley, Police Chief James Purcell, and Teamsters boss Clyde Crosby were each given the opportunity to take advantage of the newspaper's editorial space. Purcell did not accept the paper's offer, but Langley wrote a column in April 1957 that described his unfortunate situation. Langley argued, as expected, that the *Oregonian* and Elkins tried to frame him. The *Journal* also printed the first-person story of Thomas Maloney after a *Journal* reporter found the racketeer hiding out with Seattle mobster Frank Colacurcio. The *Oregonian* thought it was suspicious that a mere reporter could find a fugitive. "The answer is simple," a *Journal* editorial explained. The reporter "acted with the diligence and enterprise of a good newspaperman." "Despite its criticism," the *Journal* revealed, the *Oregonian* reprinted Maloney's story "word for word."[32]

The *Oregonian* did not let its printing presses sit idle. In an editorial column, the newspaper informed its readers of an alleged plot by the *Journal* to influence the jury for the Maloney vice racketeering trial. According to the *Oregonian*, when the judge denied a motion to suppress evidence during a pre-trial hearing, the *Journal* printed countless copies of a circular apart from its usual daily. The fliers reprinted editorials that attacked the credibility of expected witnesses in the Maloney trial. It also included a cartoon, the estimated costs of the Portland vice investigation, and a tallied score of indictments tried and dismissed. The circular was distributed to subscribers and non-subscribers and could have conceivably found its way into the boxes of potential jurors.[33]

In September 1957, the *Oregonian* released "Sorry Record of the Oregon Journal," an editorial that accused the rival newspaper of using its "truth series" and its editorial page "to tear down, destroy, or dissolve in public doubt and confusion the evidence uncovered in the *Oregonian*'s exposé of vice and corruption in Multnomah County." The *Oregonian* editors charged that the *Journal* attacked them, the state attorney general and members of his staff, the grand jury procedures, and the McClellan Committee and Robert Kennedy. The *Oregonian* was quick to point out that the *Journal*'s publisher and editor, with its chief reporter Brad Williams, were indicted on three counts of conspiracy in association with the setup of the illegal raid on Raymond Clark's home and the mishandling of evidence, meaning they made illegal copies of the King Tower tapes. The charges, however, were later dismissed on a technicality.[34]

The *Oregonian* also criticized the *Journal*'s comments about the dismissal of nearly half of the 115 indictments returned by three separate grand juries. The *Journal* suggested that the investigation by Turner and Lambert lacked credibility. "This is typical of the slanted misrepresentation to which *Journal* readers have become accustomed," an *Oregonian* editorial barked back. "This newspaper exploited a break in the underworld to bring evidence to the public of the start of a sinister syndicate here. We would have thought that a newspaper competitor would have joined in this effort, whatever its consternation at being beaten on the story."[35]

As the central figure in that story, Elkins believed that the valuable information he provided to both the *Oregonian* and as the McClellan Committee's key witness would pay off: the attention would force the corrupt Teamsters officials and Seattle racketeers out of Portland and he would regain control of the city's vice industry. Once he was informed that Kennedy and Senator McClellan would be unable to protect him from prosecution back in Portland, however, Elkins threatened to leave Washington, D.C., without testifying. "They say they can't help me," the racketeer told Turner as they stood in the middle of the street outside the Senate office building. "To hell with them, I'm gonna make a deal with the Teamsters, with Langley. . . . I'm walkin' off from all this stuff." Turner succeeded in convincing Elkins to stay.[36] In the end, Elkins and Raymond Clark were convicted of violating federal wiretapping laws for creating the King Tower tapes. The racketeers received rather light sentences and fines. Elkins was sentenced to serve twenty months and to pay $2,000 in fines. Clark was sentenced to serve six months and was fined $500.[37]

Not satisfied with this outcome, Elkins, Clark, and their lawyers appealed to the Ninth Circuit Court and argued that their conviction in federal court was based on evidence that a district court judge had suppressed on the grounds that the King Tower tapes had been illegally seized from Clark's home. Moreover, their convictions were also based on the testimony of the same law enforcement officials, particularly William Langley, who, the local judge ruled, seized the tapes illegally. In fact, in March 1960, Langley, now no longer acting as district attorney, but as a lawyer in private practice, argued in federal court supporting the so-called "silver platter" doctrine, a law that allowed federal officials to use evidence illegally obtained by local law enforcement officials. The argument was successful and the circuit court denied Elkins and Clark their appeal.[38]

Despite the fact that Elkins and Clark were vice racketeers, there is some evidence that indicates the *Oregonian* newspaper and federal officials did everything they could to protect the two defendants from prosecution. *Oregonian* editor Robert Notson and the newspaper's attorney David Fain told Oregon Attorney General Robert Thornton in 1956 that the newspaper promised protection to Elkins and Raymond Clark, and that it would not give the attorney general access to the tape recordings unless he guaranteed the racketeers' immunity from prosecution on wiretapping violations. According to Thornton, he explained to Notson and Fain that he did not have the authority to protect Elkins and Clark from federal prosecution.[39] Nonetheless, Wallace Turner maintains that the *Oregonian* paid for the racketeers' defense in the ensuing trial and their appeal to the Ninth Circuit Court.[40]

U.S. Attorney General Robert Kennedy also had reason to try to protect the racketeers from federal prosecution. According to Kennedy and Senator McClellan, James Elkins made a great sacrifice by helping their labor racketeering investigation. Kennedy met Elkins for the first time in December 1956 and described him as "a slim, rugged-looking man with a rather kindly face and a very attractive and devoted wife." Although Elkins was "reluctant to talk" at their first meeting, later, after he decided to cooperate, he spoke freely with the chief counsel.[41] "Because his background was so unsavory," Kennedy later reported, "we checked his story up and down, backward and forward, inside and out. We found he didn't lie, and that he didn't exaggerate."[42] As Wallace Turner later explained, Kennedy handled his source with consummate skill. "It was plain to me . . . that Bob [Kennedy] knew . . . how to deal with . . . a nefarious source." Kennedy "understood that one must be honest with [Elkins] . . . that with those people, honesty is first and foremost." In fact, during the senate investigation, Kennedy and Elkins ultimately became very cordial. "Elkins seemed to like Bob, and that, of course, was terribly important," Turner later reported.[43]

Both Kennedy and Elkins benefited from this cordial relationship. According to FBI documents, U.S. Attorney Judson Bowles telephoned the Portland special agent in charge in April 1961 and emphasized that Elkins was "a very excellent and cooperative witness before the McClellan Committee at the time that Attorney General Kennedy was Chief Counsel and that Mr. McClellan had practically insisted that the Department [of Justice] not prosecute Elkins." Nonetheless, U.S. Attorney Bowles indicated that Elkins was "a top racketeer" and that he was proceeding in the prosecution of Elkins under the Unauthorized Publication or Use of Communications statute.[44]

After losing in the appellate court, Elkins and Clark appealed to the U.S. Supreme Court. When the *Oregonian* withdrew its financial and thus legal support, Turner recalled, Kennedy apparently stepped in and became Elkins's advocate. "Why did the *Oregonian* turn its back on Jim?" Robert Kennedy later asked Wallace Turner. Having already left the *Oregonian*, the reporter was not aware that the newspaper had discontinued its financial support of Elkins and Clark. Turner then wondered who financed the racketeer's appeal to the Supreme Court. Kennedy explained, "My brothers and I paid for it." According to Turner, Kennedy felt "obligated" to help Elkins knowing of the racketeer's abuse of alcohol and narcotics, and the "great personal sacrifice" he had made for the McClellan Committee.[45] The Portland vice scandal, and especially James Elkins, helped Kennedy make his case against the Teamsters, and that was Kennedy's overriding priority.

The U.S. Supreme Court agreed to hear Elkins's case, and in its June 1960 decision, overruled the "silver platter" doctrine. The justices agreed that the raid on Clark's home violated the defendant's Fourth Amendment protection against illegal search and seizure. They set aside the judgment of the appellate court and sent the case back to the district court. [46] Once the case was thrown back to Portland, Attorney General Kennedy continued to help Elkins and Clark. At his Hickory Hill home in Virginia, Kennedy ordered U.S. Attorney for Oregon Sidney Lezak to fire Deputy U.S. Attorney David Robinson for his enthusiastic prosecution of the Portland racketeer. Many years later, Lezak recalled how he refused to punish Robinson and would not allow the attorney general to dictate how he should run his office in Oregon.[47] Nevertheless, according to FBI documents, U.S. Attorney Lezak told agents in Portland that the pending indictments against Elkins and Clark were dismissed by the U.S. District Court on September 26, 1961, "upon motion of U.S. Department of Justice."[48] Thus, Attorney General Robert Kennedy ultimately was able to protect Elkins from prosecution.

While he enjoyed this protection from Kennedy and other law enforcement officials, given the nature of his business, James Elkins could not be protected from threats of violence by former associates. After he stopped cooperating with the Seattle group and the Teamsters in 1956, union thugs constantly harassed Elkins and his wife, Colleen. Elkins later told Robert Kennedy that he and his wife frequently received anonymous and threatening telephone calls in the middle of the night. One night a caller threatened, "We are just a minute away and we are coming to break both arms and both legs." This, according to Kennedy, was what convinced Elkins to bug the King Tower apartment and take the recordings to Wallace Turner at the *Oregonian*.[49]

On November 25, 1959, Colleen Elkins telephoned Senate investigator Arthur Kaplan and provided him with details about a call that she received earlier that day from Detroit. Mrs. Elkins told Kaplan that the call was from Jimmy Hoffa, who recently spoke to her father, Murray Gamrath, a Multnomah County investigator. According to Mrs. Elkins, Hoffa was looking for her husband. After she told him that her husband was unavailable to speak with him, he asked whether her husband told her everything about his business. "Well, do *you* confide in *your* wife?" she asked. "Only those things I wish her to know," Hoffa replied. Hoffa then asked her whether her husband ever discussed leaving the country. Elkins later disclosed that Hoffa offered him "a sum of money and a passport to leave the country." Elkins claimed that he had received calls from Hoffa and other Teamsters officials at least five times since the McClellan Committee hearings began in 1957. According to Elkins, these officials tried to convince him to travel and talk with them face-to-face. He always refused, the racketeer maintained, knowing that they would most likely kill him. Elkins asserted that "in every instance" he was offered money and "advance fare to make the trip."[50]

Once the attention of the McClellan Committee hearings and the local criminal investigations and trials died down, Elkins attempted to pick up his business where he left off. The city, especially Mayor Terry Schrunk and the police bureau, however, kept close tabs on the racketeer. He was arrested in 1959 with Clark and safecracker Harry Huerth (King) in Beaverton while allegedly staking out and planning the robbery of a Safeway and a Raleigh Hills Kienow grocery store. The charges against the robbery crew were dropped.[51] According to former U.S. Attorney Sidney Lezak, they were dismissed because Elkins blackmailed the judge with information that exposed his alleged homosexual acts.[52]

With his Portland syndicate drying up, Elkins left the Rose City in 1968 and the available information regarding his activities and his demise is scarce and sketchy. According to one report, he traveled to Globe, Arizona, to start a new operation there. The plan, however, never got off the ground, for shortly after he arrived, the 67-year-old racketeer was killed in a traffic accident. An autopsy revealed that Elkins suffered a heart attack just before his automobile hit a utility pole.[53] According to another report, however, a few officers in the Portland Police Bureau became suspicious after Elkins's body was cremated immediately. One officer actually traveled to Arizona and allegedly returned to Portland with a morgue photograph that showed the aged vice racketeer was murdered—shot twice in the chest.[54]

Historians of the Progressive Era located this reform movement as a response to rapid urbanization at the turn of the twentieth century, and urbanization was the byproduct of industrialization and the sharp increase in immigration and internal migration. The subsequent problems of urban society—increased crime, law enforcement corruption, and inadequate social welfare programs—prompted a host of political reforms including a direct primary, referendums, recalls, initiatives, city managers, and commission governments. These reforms were adopted to combat corrupt political machines and enforce social morality.

Many cities in the 1950s resembled the turn-of-the-century cities: crime-filled and corrupt. Accordingly, attempts at reform during the twentieth century were limited and had few results, and Portland was no exception. Reformers in Philadelphia, St. Louis, Chicago, and New York battled police graft, organized crime, and political corruption in the early years of the twentieth century. In the 1920s and 1930s, the same battles were fought, and for the most part lost, in Los Angeles, San Francisco, and Chicago. By the 1950s, these and other large cities experienced a resurgence of corruption and organized crime, which was exacerbated by labor racketeering.

In 1959, Oregon Attorney General Robert Thornton concluded that the Portland vice investigation and the McClellan hearings exposed "a very bad payoff situation which had existed in the Portland police department. . . . Obviously, these illicit bootleg and gambling establishments and houses of prostitution could not have operated without official protection. Those things just do not operate without official protection." The subsequent public attention, the attorney general later explained, led to "cleaning up all the illicit bootlegging establishments . . . closed down the houses of prostitution . . . [and led to a] good house cleaning in the district attorney's office."[55]

Wallace Turner later explained that once James Elkins was involved with the *Oregonian*, everything closed down. He was "hotter than a firecracker" and no other vice racketeers wanted to deal with him. In fact, Chuck Bollinger, a Portland police officer from the late 1960s to the late 1980s, explained that vice crime was not as open and public in the mid-1960s as it had been a decade before. As a member of the Portland Police Bureau's Intelligence Division, Bollinger and his partners used surveillance equipment and other covert methods to investigate vice crime.[56] In 1948, the City Club investigators walked down the street and into brothels to collect their data on prostitution and gambling in Portland demonstrating the availability of illegal entertainment and the openness of these operations.

Attorney General Robert Thornton had the hindsight in 1959 to predict the pattern of Portland's vice industry. "The history of these things is that the underworld merely bides its time and waits until the attention of the public and of the law enforcement agencies are concentrated in another direction and then [once] again they seek to move in and take over things."[57] In fact, by the mid-1970s, Frank Colacurcio Jr., heir to the Colacurcio family vice ring in Seattle, was expanding his prostitution and other criminal activities into

Portland.[58] At the same time, the Portland Police Bureau struggled with graft. As a rookie cop in the 1970s, former Portland Police Chief Charles Moose was routinely exposed to intense situations involving violence, drugs, and vice in downtown Portland. Many inexperienced officers, Moose recalled, fell over to the "dark side" of criminal conduct by taking bribes or profiting from criminal activity.[59] An underpaid police bureau and the lack of political leadership made Portland attractive again to organized crime figures, and the principal contributors to Portland's municipal crime problem, as in many cities, were racketeers who cultivated relationships with municipal officials and law enforcement officers.

Portland provides the basis for a broader understanding of issues of urban corruption and crime in American cities. The multitude and variety of sources available on municipal and criminal activities in Portland provide incredible insight into how labor, business, and government operated in the "open city" of the twentieth century. This important, though dystopian, segment of Portland's history serves to help explain the rapid growth and mismanagement of American cities, the prevalence and magnitude of labor racketeering, and the development and influence of organized crime on local law enforcement and politicians. "Beneath all the lovely lawns and rose gardens," former *Oregonian* reporter Wallace Turner later described, "there was an immense amount of corruption [in Portland]."[60]

ABBREVIATIONS

AKP   Arthur Kaplan Papers
ERP   Earl Riley Papers
JMP   John McClellan Papers
OBU   Ouachita Baptist University
OHSRL   Oregon Historical Society Research Library

NOTES

INTRODUCTION

1   Vice crime is described here as anything associated with gambling, boot-legging, and prostitution. Racketeering is the coordinated planning and execution of crimes, and through bribery, racketeers often greased the palms of law enforcement officials—police, district attorneys, and even mayors—to facilitate the implementation of widespread vice operations.

2   Senate, Select Committee on Improper Activities in the Labor or Management Field, *Interim Report*, 85th Congress, 2d sess., March 24, 1958, S. Rep. 1417, 39. Hereafter *Interim Report*.

3   *Time*, April 8, 1957, 67.

4   Law Library of Congress, "American Women: Immigration." Available online at http://memory.loc.gov/ammem/awhhtml/awlaw3/ immigration.html (accessed September 26, 2010); Myers, *Municipal Mother*, 80, 96–97.

5   MacColl, *Growth of a City*, 6.

6   *Oregon Journal*, August 24, 1912, 4.

7   Hofstadter, *Age of Reform*, 257.

8   Ibid., 182.

9   Berner, *Seattle 1900–1920*, 5.

10   Ibid.

11   Haller, "Urban Crime and Criminal Justice," 619–35.

12   Ibid.

13   Ibid.

14   *Report and Proceedings of the Senate Committee Appointed to Investigate*

the *Police Department of the City of New York*, vol. 1, 1895, in *New York City Police Corruption Investigation Commissions, 1894–1994*, ed. Gabriel J. Chin, 3–8; Dunlop, *Gilded City*, 17.

15 "Third Interim Report of the Special Committee to Investigate Organized Crime in Interstate Commerce," in *Theft of the City*, eds. Gardner and Olson, 68–72.

16 "Law Enforcement in Portland and Multnomah County," *City Club of Portland Bulletin*, February 1948.

17 Lichtenstein, *State of the Union*, 54, 142.

18 The King Tower tapes were recorded in the King Tower apartments, located on Southwest King Avenue, off West Burnside in downtown Portland.

19 Quote from editorial title, *Oregonian*, January 24, 1947, 10.

1. EARLY PORTLAND AND THE FAILURE OF PROGRESSIVE REFORM

1 Schwantes, *Pacific Northwest*, 194–95; Abbott, *Portland*, 11.

2 MacColl, *Shaping of a City*, 5.

3 Abbott, *Portland*, 2.

4 DeMarco, *Short History of Portland*, 43.

5 Gardner and Olson, *Theft of the City*, 40.

6 Lansing, *Portland*, 178.

7 Ibid., 178–80; MacColl, *Merchants, Money, and Power*, 219–20.

8 Steffens, *Shame of the Cities*, 7.

9 Ibid., 6.

10 Gardiner and Olson, *Theft of the City*, 41–42.

11 Abbott, *Portland*, 55.

12 MacColl, *Merchants, Money, and Power*, 291.

13 Reed, *Municipal Government in the United States*, 91–92.

14 Qtd. in Reed, *Municipal Government in the United States*, 98.

15 MacColl, *Merchants, Money, and Power*, 170–72.

16 Ibid., 322.

17 In the 1870s, the official ratio of silver to gold was 16 to 1, meaning sixteen ounces of silver equaled one ounce of gold. Therefore, silver owners took their metal to manufacturers rather than to the mint. Congress recognized this and discontinued the coinage of silver in 1873. Pro-silver Republicans and Democrats campaigned for free, unlimited coinage of silver, believing it was a solution to the nation's currency problem (dwindling gold reserves had devalued paper money) and the economic depression.

18 MacColl, *Merchants, Money, and Power*, 322.

19 Qtd. in MacColl, *Merchants, Money, and Power*, 369.

20 Leeson, *Rose City Justice*, 68; Lansing, *Portland*, 261; MacColl, *Merchants, Money, and Power*, 369–71.

21   Leeson, *Rose City Justice*, 36; MacColl, *Merchants, Money, and Power*, 218, 244.
22   Lansing, *Portland*, 185–86, 250.
23   MacColl, *Shaping of a City*, 60, 64, 195.
24   Lansing, *Portland*, 203; MacColl, *Merchants, Money, and Power*, 193.
25   MacColl, *Merchants, Money, and Power*, 290.
26   New York's Committee of Fourteen was founded in 1905 by reformers who wanted "Raines Laws" hotels closed because they spread prostitution. The Raines Law of 1896 allowed hotels to serve alcohol on Sundays, while saloons were closed. Saloon owners, therefore, annexed hotels or built rooms and applied for hotel liquor licenses. The rooms were then often used for prostitution. Yoles, Committee of Fourteen Records, 1905–1932.
27   MacColl, *Merchants, Money, and Power*, 290–91; MacColl, *Shaping of a City*, 195–96.
28   Ibid.
29   Lansing, *Portland*, 208.
30   MacColl, *Merchants, Money, and Power*, 321.
31   Perkins, "Here and There: Volume I."
32   Ibid.
33   Lansing, *Portland*, 244.
34   MacColl, *Merchants, Money, and Power*, 341–42.
35   Clement, *Love For Sale*, 80.
36   Wong, *Sweet Cakes, Long Journey*, 131.
37   Johnston, *Radical Middle Class*, xi.
38   Myers, *Municipal Mother*, 7.
39   Lansing, *Portland*, 262.
40   Ibid., 269.
41   Myers, *Municipal Mother*, 6; MacColl, *Shaping of a City*, 315, 327.
42   *Oregon Journal*, January 17, 1906, 1–2, 4; *Oregon Journal*, January 18, 1906, 1; *Oregon Journal*, January 19, 1906, 2; *Oregon Journal*, January 21, 1906, 1.
43   *Oregon Journal*, January 18, 1906, 1.
44   MacColl, *Shaping of a City*, 327.
45   Lansing, *Portland*, 270–72.
46   Johnston, *Radical Middle Class*, 95; MacColl, *Shaping of the City*, 377, 399, 401.
47   Lansing, *Portland*, 279; MacColl, *Shaping of the City*, 401.
48   Talbot, *Report of the Portland Vice Commission to the Mayor of the City of Portland, Oregon, January 1913*, 2.
49   Ibid., 68.
50   *Oregonian*, August 24, 1912, 6; see also *Oregonian*, August 23, 1912, 1.
51   MacColl, *Shaping of a City*, 405.
52   Ibid.
53   Ibid., 408.

54 Lansing, *Portland*, 283–84; MacColl, *Shaping of a City*, 408.
55 *Oregon Journal*, August 26, 1912, 1.
56 *Oregon Journal*, August 24, 1912, 3.
57 MacColl, *Shaping of a City*, 409.
58 Clement, *Love For Sale*, 86.
59 MacColl, *Shaping of a City*, 411–12; Lansing, *Portland*, 287.
60 Bureau of Municipal Research, New York City, *Organization and Business Methods of the City Government of Portland, Oregon*, 5.
61 Ibid., 28, 36.
62 Ibid., 68, 73.
63 "The 1900 Storm," *Galveston Daily News*, 2008. Available online at http://www.1900storm.com (accessed September 27, 2010).
64 Johnston, *Radical Middle Class*, 97.
65 MacColl, *Shaping of a City*, 459.
66 Ibid.
67 Ibid., 459–60.
68 MacColl, *Growth of a City*, 276.
69 Marsh, *20 Years A Soldier of Fortune*, 181.
70 Ibid., 182.
71 Ibid., 187.
72 MacColl, *Growth of a City*, 277–78.
73 Mullins, *Depression and the Urban West Coast, 1929–1933*, 1, 17.
74 Letter, Martha Allen to Commissioner Dorothy Lee, January 12, 1945, Box 4, ERP, MSS 1123, OHSRL, Portland; Letter, U. F. Heinbeck to Dr. I. George Nace, April 2, 1944, Box 4, ERP, MSS 1123, OHSRL, Portland; Department of Records to Chief of Police, March 2, 1948, Box 6, ERP, MSS 1123, OHSRL, Portland; Portland Police Survey, 1947, Box 6, ERP, MSS 1123, OHSRL, Portland; "Law Enforcement in Portland and Multnomah County," *City Club of Portland Bulletin*.

2. POST—WORLD WAR II PORTLAND

1 *Oregonian*, January 24, 1947, 10; MacColl, *Growth of a City*, 647–48; Pitzer, "Dorothy McCullough Lee," 13; *Portland Tribune*, June 1, 2001, 1. Available online at http://www.portlandtribune.com/archview. cgi?id=4058 (accessed May 28, 2002). The FBI called Elkins the "vice czar." Memo, SAC Portland to Rosen, July 13, 1960, FBI 139-373-240.
2 Democrat Raymond Tucker served St. Louis as mayor from 1953 to 1965 and was most widely known for improvements to the city's infrastructure and urban renewal programs. Seattle's Bertha Landes served a short term as mayor from 1926 until 1928, and is celebrated for her attempt at "municipal housekeeping," attacking law enforcement corruption and the vice industry. Frank Ziedler, Milwaukee's Socialist mayor, held the post from 1948 to 1960, although he continued to serve the city well beyond his time in city hall. He improved fire service and

garbage collection, but is most remembered for his attention to Milwaukee's impoverished neighborhoods. David Lawrence was elected mayor of Pittsburgh in 1945 and spent his next fourteen years in city hall leading the city through a renaissance. Lawrence's most notable achievement was his successful attack on Pittsburgh's infamous smog. At 5'2", Fiorello LaGuardia wielded the authority of a giant. As mayor of New York from 1934 to 1945, LaGuardia modernized and greatly improved city government, transportation, housing, and schools. Although he was a Republican, he became one of New York's greatest mayors because he moved beyond party politics to improve city life. For example, he embraced many of Franklin Roosevelt's New Deal programs.

3   Mullins, *Depression and the Urban West Coast, 1929–1933*, 1, 17.

4   Lucia, *Conscience of a City*, 22.

5   Gardiner and Olson, *Theft of the City*, 41.

6   MacColl, *Growth of a City*, 612; Abbott, *Portland*, 117–18.

7   MacColl, *Growth of a City*, 609.

8   "Is Earl Riley a Fit Man for Mayor?" Box 2, ERP, MSS 1123, OHSRL, Portland.

9   Lansing, *Portland*, 322–33; MacColl, *Growth of a City*, 493–94.

10 "Is Earl Riley a Fit Man for Mayor?"

11 Ibid.; MacColl, *Growth of a City*, 615.

12 MacColl, *Growth of a City*, 615.

13 Abbott, *Portland*, 131.

14 Ibid., 126.

15 Ibid., 136.

16 U.S. Department of Commerce, Bureau of the Census, "Wartime Changes in Population and Family Characteristics," 1–3; Abbott, *Portland*, 125–31.

17 MacColl, *Growth of a City*, 613.

18 Abbott, *Portland*, 129.

19 Letter, Martha Allen to Commissioner Dorothy Lee, January 12, 1945, Box 4, ERP, MSS 1123, OHSRL, Portland; Letter, U. F. Heinbeck to Dr. I. George Nace, April 2, 1944, Box 4, ERP, MSS 1123, OHSRL, Portland.

20 Department of Records to Chief of Police, March 2, 1948, Box 6, ERP, MSS 1123, OHSRL, Portland; Portland Police Survey, 1947, Box 6, ERP, MSS 1123, OHSRL, Portland. When considering the scope of Riley's corruption, it is important to consider that police reports alone are insufficient to assess the effectiveness of Riley's brief reform efforts. The only record of vice violations was that of arrests as no reports were written unless an arrest was made. Furthermore, "victims" of vice crime rarely filed complaints of criminal activity unless they suffered harm or injury as a consequence of the activity. Naturally, victims avoided publicizing their participation. Vollmer, "Portland Bureau Survey," 21, OHSRL, Portland.

21 Abbott, *Portland*, 118.
22 Letter, Mayor Earl Riley to Ben H. Hazen, September 4, 1945, Box 4, ERP, MSS 1123, OHSRL, Portland.
23 MacColl, *Growth of a City*, 610, 647.
24 In New York City, the Committee of Fourteen (and later Fifteen) investigated prostitution and pressured owners and managers to clean up their properties by threatening suppliers and insurance providers. Clement, *Love for Sale*, 10–11.
25 Lucia, *Conscious of a City*, 11–12, 61.
26 "Portland's Public Health Enemy Number One," *City Club of Portland Bulletin*, January 1945.
27 Reckless, "The Impact of War on Crime, Delinquency, and Prostitution," 378–86.
28 "Portland's Public Health Enemy Number One."
29 Police Survey, 1947, Box 6, ERP, MSS 1123, OHSRL, Portland.
30 Officer's Report, January 9, 1942, Box 5, ERP, MSS 1123, OHSRL, Portland.
31 "Portland's Public Health Enemy Number One."
32 Ibid.
33 Clement, *Love for Sale*, 77.
34 "Portland's Public Health Enemy Number One."
35 "Law Enforcement in Portland and Multnomah County," *City Club of Portland Bulletin,* February 1948.
36 Ibid.
37 Ibid.
38 Letter, Mrs. Eugene Kinnicutt to Mayor Earl Riley, September 5, 1947, Box 6, ERP, MSS 1123, OHSRL, Portland.
39 Portland Trade Union Bureau to Mayor Earl Riley and City Council, n.d., Box 6, ERP, MSS 1123, OHSRL, Portland.
40 Letter, Mayor Earl Riley to Ben H. Hazen, September 4, 1945, Box 4, ERP, MSS 1123, OHSRL, Portland.
41 Vollmer, "Portland Bureau Survey," 23.
42 "Law Enforcement in Portland and Multnomah County."
43 Chambliss, *On the Take*, 35–37.
44 Ibid., 134.
45 MacColl, *Growth of a City*, 614. In 2001, MacColl told the author that while touring city hall with Dorothy McCullough Lee, the former mayor showed him the secret vault and she explained that Riley circulated bribe money in and out of the safe.
46 Robert F. Kennedy, handwritten notes, n.d., Robert F. Kennedy Papers, John F. Kennedy Library, Boston, Massachusetts. Al Winter was the most successful vice operator in Portland during the Depression and in the 1940s. Winter was the son of a judge and a lawyer himself, but was a heavyweight in bootlegging and gambling. After Prohibition was repealed, the criminals who had their first taste

as bootleggers successfully came to organize and control the other vices—such as gambling and prostitution. Winter reportedly controlled Portland's gambling rackets out of the Pago Pago, a club on Southwest Stark Street downtown. Winter also operated the Turf Club Race Room, where his activities were uninterrupted as long as he continued to bribe police officers and officials at city hall. Officer's Report, Oregon State Police, May 30, 1956; Stanford, *Portland Confidential*, 23.

47 *Oregonian*, February 20, 1948, 1, 13.
48 Letter, Mayor Earl Riley to Rev. Harry C. Holtze, April 3, 1946, Box 4, ERP, MSS 1123, OHSRL, Portland.
49 Letter, Mayor Earl Riley to H. R. Dinger, April 3, 1946, Box 4, ERP, MSS 1123, OHSRL, Portland.
50 Ibid.
51 "Law Enforcement in Portland and Multnomah County."
52 Ibid.
53 Ibid.
54 Officer's Report, January 9, 1942, Box 5, ERP, MSS 1123, OHSRL, Portland; MacColl, *Growth of a City*, 609.
55 "Law Enforcement in Portland and Multnomah County."
56 Memo, SAC Portland to Rosen, July 13, 1960, FBI 139-373-240.
57 *State of Oregon v. James B. Elkins*, September 24, 1956, Circuit Court of the State of Oregon for Multnomah County, Multnomah County Courthouse, Records, case no. 34333.
58 Stanley Terry, interview by Linda Brody, 1982, SC 9511, Stanley Terry Oral History Collection, tape 92T3295 B1982, nos. 1–2, transcript, 6–7, OHSRL, Portland. Hereafter referred to as Terry oral history.
59 Senate, Select Committee on Investigations, *Hearings on Investigation of Improper Activities in the Labor or Management Field*, 85th Cong., 1st sess., February 26, 1957, 494. Hereafter referred to as *Hearings*.
60 King, *Box Man*, 61.
61 Officer's Report, Oregon State Police, June 29, 1956.
62 King, *Box Man*, 16, 63.
63 Ibid., 60.
64 Ibid., 17.
65 Ibid., 61.
66 The Federal Bureau of Narcotics was established by the Department of Treasury in 1930. It was later merged with the Bureau of Drug Abuse Control in 1968 and housed in the Food and Drug Administration.
67 Turner, interview with author, August 5, 2003. Hereafter referred to as Turner interview.
68 *Hearings*, 74.
69 King, *Box Man*, 61.
70 *Hearings*, 494.
71 Officer's Report, Oregon State Police, June 29, 1956.
72 *Portland Tribune*, August 23, 2002, C6.

73 King, *Box Man*, 61.

74 Terry oral history, 24.

75 Officer's Report, Oregon State Police, June 29, 1956.

76 King, *Box Man*, 62–63.

77 Terry oral history, 13–14.

78 King, *Box Man*, 64–65.

79 Abbott, *Portland*, 147–48.

80 Ibid., 155–57; Berman and Merrill, "Citizens Attitudes toward Municipal Reform Institutions," 274–83.

81 Scott Lee, untitled biography of Dorothy McCullough Lee, Dorothy Lee Papers, MSS 2772, OHSRL, Portland.

82 Ibid.

83 Pitzer, "Dorothy McCullough Lee," 5, 14–15.

84 Ibid., 16.

85 Ibid., 23.

86 Turner interview.

87 Lee, untitled biography of Dorothy McCullough Lee. Gambling machine distributor Stan Terry said that many people tried to connect Portland with eastern Mafia families because the gambling devices used in the West usually came from Chicago. But according to Harry King, the syndicates in the West were local organizations and did not extend beyond Portland. Terry oral history, 21; King, *Box Man*, 75.

88 *Oregonian*, December 25, 1950, 16.

89 Pitzer, "Dorothy McCullough Lee," 16. Punchboards were cardboard panels that had hundreds of small holes covered with paper. A gambler would pay the operator (the bet was usually a nickel) for the chance to use a metal pin to "punch" a hole and pull out a piece of paper that listed a prize, usually a toy or candy, but sometimes cash.

90 *Oregonian*, December 25, 1950, 16.

91 Ibid.; Pitzer, "Dorothy McCullough Lee," 16–17, 25.

92 Portland City Council Minutes, April 12, 1951, City of Portland Stanley Parr Archives and Records Center, Portland, Oregon.

93 Portland City Council Minutes, April 4, 1951, City of Portland Stanley Parr Archives and Records Center, Portland, Oregon.

94 Lee, untitled biography of Dorothy McCullough Lee.

95 Ibid.; Pitzer, "Dorothy McCullough Lee," 25.

96 Pitzer, "Dorothy McCullough Lee," 16, 29.

97 Lansing, *Portland*, 362.

98 Pitzer, "Dorothy McCullough Lee," 30.

99 MacColl, *Growth of a City*, 649; Lansing, *Portland*, 362.

100 Abbott, *Portland*, 159. Peterson had not been Lee's ally on the city council; in April 1951, he had successfully delayed one of the mayor's anti-vice ordinances by requesting further study and amendments to the legislation. Portland City Council Minutes, April 4, 1951.

101 *Oregonian*, August 3, 1953, 1.

102 Ibid.; *State of Oregon v. James B. Elkins*, September 24, 1956, Circuit Court of the State of Oregon for Multnomah County, Multnomah County Courthouse, Records, case 34333.

103 *Oregon Journal*, April 9, 1957, 1.

104 Ibid.

105 Officer's Report, Oregon State Police, May 2, 1956; *Oregon Journal*, April 9, 1957, 2. One year later, Captain Mariels told the *Oregon Journal* that having learned of the reporter's interest in "background information for a book," he had personally arranged the meeting between the *Oregonian*'s Miller and Elkins. The captain claimed to have been "flabbergasted" that Elkins had tried to bribe and threaten Miller. According to an *Oregon Journal* report, Miller advised his editors at the *Oregonian* of his discoveries and a portion of his story, edited to protect Patrolman Olsen, was forwarded to Multnomah County District Attorney William Langley. However, while the newspaper editors waited for some action, Langley did nothing. It appears that the *Oregonian* was quite unaware of the racketeer's arrangements with local law enforcement officials, which included, coincidentally, District Attorney Langley. Finally, the *Oregon Journal* printed the story after, according to the *Journal*'s editors, the *Oregonian* was too embarrassed to disclose their naïveté. *Oregon Journal*, April 9, 1957, 2.

106 King, *Box Man*, 65.

107 MacColl, *Growth of a City*, 655.

3. ELKINS VS. THE TEAMSTERS

1 King Tower tapes, transcript, AKP, private collection; *Hearings*, 535.

2 *Hearings*, 80, 104.

3 Brill, *Teamsters*, 14–30; Baltakis, "Agendas of Investigation," 414–18.

4 Dubofsky, *State and Labor in Modern America*, 37–38.

5 Russell, *Out of the Jungle*, 33, 43.

6 Garnel, *Rise of Teamster Power in the West*, 40.

7 Lichtenstein, *State of the Union*, 163.

8 Brill, *Teamsters*, 14.

9 Lichtenstein, *State of the Union*, 142.

10 Garnel, *Rise of Teamster Power in the West*, 86.

11 McCallum, *Dave Beck*, 5, 18, 38–40, 47–49. Dave Beck was born in 1894 in Stockton, California, but moved to Seattle with his family when he was four. He grew up in the Belltown neighborhood, but at age nine, the family moved into his father's carpet shop on Pike Street. As a young boy, he roamed the streets shooting rats—earning five dollars for every kill from the Seattle Health Department—and delivered the morning *Post-Intelligencer* and the evening *Seattle Times*. When he was seventeen, he played semi-pro baseball around Seattle, and when

the U.S. entered the Great War, Beck joined the Navy and was sent to England as a machinist's mate.

12 Ibid., 54.

13 Ibid., 55, 65, 75.

14 Telegram, Hood to Rosen, June 2, 1949, FBI 6-128-7, 86–87.

15 A dray is a cart with no sides.

16 Carole Beers, "Frank Brewster, Teamsters Leader—Union Powerhouse Had Worked His Way Up Through Ranks," *The Seattle Times*, November 21, 1996, B4.

17 *New York Journal-American*, September 14, 1956, 17.

18 *Oregon Teamster*, March 28, 1957, 1–7.

19 Correlation Summary, March 26, 1964, FBI 122-1812-18; Memo, Director to SAC Seattle, June 6, 1960, FBI 159-206-4.

20 Ibid.

21 Letter, SAC Seattle R. D. Auerbach to Assistant. Director Lou Nichols, October 16, 1956, FBI 122-1812-17; Kennedy, *Enemy Within*, 258; Officer's Report, Oregon State Police, May 10, 1956. Frank Colacurcio Sr., was the patriarch of the infamous Colacurcio family, an organization often compared to those in Chicago, Miami, Philadelphia, and New York. Colacurcio started in the gambling and vending machine rackets in the 1950s and then quickly moved into prostitution. As late as the 1980s, federal and local law enforcement investigated Colacurcio and his son, Frank Jr., for prostitution in connection with his profitable strip-club businesses, which operated in ten western states. In 1971, the elder Colacurcio was convicted of bribing police to ignore illegal gambling in his taverns. In June 2008, the Colacurcios were again under investigation, this time for the murders of five people, executed in the 1970s and 1980s allegedly for double-crossing the Seattle mobsters. Steve Miletich and Jim Brunner, "The Cops vs. Colacurcio—The Last Round," *The Seattle Times*, June 13, 2008, available online at http://seattletimes.nwsource.com/html/localnews/2003695542_colacurcio06m.html (accessed October 19, 2010); see also *The Seattle Times*, May 6, 2007, A1.

22 *Interim Report*, 35; *Hearings*, 17, 57–58, 67, 81, 372.

23 *Hearings*, 150–56, 426.

24 *Time*, "The Terrifying Teamsters," March 11, 1957, 18.

25 *Hearings*, 17, 57–58, 67, 81, 372; Officer's Report, Oregon State Police, May 10, 1956.

26 *Time*, "The Terrifying Teamsters," 18.

27 *Hearings*, 17, 57–58, 67, 81, 372; Officer's Report, Oregon State Police, May 10, 1956.

28 Letter, Auerbach to Nichols, October 16, 1956, FBI 122-1812-17; Letter, Robert Kennedy to Bernard Nossiter (*Washington Post*), April 16, 1957, Robert F. Kennedy Pre-Administration Papers, John F. Kennedy Library, Boston, Massachusetts.

29   *Interim Report*, 9.

30   Terry oral history; *Hearings*, 246–47; Officer's Report, Oregon State
      Police, May 16, 1956.

31   *Oregonian*, December 25, 1950, 16.; Lee, untitled biography of Dorothy
      McCullough Lee; Leeson, *Rose City Justice*, 145.

32   Uris, "Trouble in River City," 221.

33   Officer's Report, Oregon State Police, June 16, 1956.

34   Lansing, *Portland*, 349, 374; Uris, "Trouble in River City," 60, 198.

35   *Hearings*, 161; U.S. Congress, *McClellan Committee Hearings: 1957*, 13,
      163, 326. This is a day-to-day report of the Senate's investigation of
      labor racketeering and other abuses by union leaders, fully indexed and
      keyed to the official record of the hearings.

36   *Oregon Journal*, February 23, 1956, 10.

37   Statement of Receipts and Expenditures, O'Donnell for City Commis-
      sioner, Office of the City Auditor, Portland, Oregon, May 18, 1956.

38   *Interim Report*, 14; *Hearings*, 139, 141; Kennedy, *Enemy Within*, 259.

39   Memo, Conversation with Budge Wright, May 23, 1956, AKP, private
      collection.

40   *Hearings*, 184, 198. In his testimony before the McClellan Committee,
      Lloyd Hildreth, secretary of Portland Teamsters Local 223, claimed
      that Clyde Crosby, an organizer for the International Brotherhood of
      Teamsters, took the unusual step of ordering the pickets at the Mount
      Hood Café.

41   Ibid., 185.

42   Correlation Summary, March 26, 1964, FBI 122-1812-18; Memo, Robert
      F. Kennedy to Arthur Kaplan, April 4, 1958, AKP, private collection.

43   *Hearings*, 81.

44   Officer's Report, Oregon State Police, May 31, 1956.

45   *Hearings*, 934.

46   Application Qualified Restaurant License, Oregon Liquor Control
      Commission, September 8, 1949; *Oregonian*, April 25, 1956, 1; *Orego-
      nian*, May 20, 1956, 12, AKP, private collection.

47   *Interim Report*, 9.

48   Officer's Report, Oregon State Police, May 31, 1956.

49   *Interim Report*, 11.

50   *Hearings*, 91, 104–7; Letter, Kennedy to Nossiter; Officer's Report,
      Oregon State Police, May 31, 1956.

51   *Hearings*, 86, 109–12.

52   *Oregon Teamster*, March 28, 1957, 6.

53   *Hearings*, 315–16.

54   Ibid., 333; King Tower tapes, audio recordings, no. 3, September 1955.

55   *Hearings*, 320.

56   *Interim Report*, 25–26.

57   King Tower tapes, audio recordings, no. 4, September 1955.

58   *Interim Report*, 25–26.

59 King Tower tapes, audio recordings, no. 3, September 1955.

60 Kennedy, *Enemy Within*, 261; *Hearings*, 535.

61 King Tower tapes, transcript, AKP, private collection; *Hearings*, 535.

62 Officer's Report, Oregon State Police, June 19, 1956.

63 *State of Oregon v. William Langley et al.*, July 31, 1956, case no. 34316; *Interim Report*, 40; King Tower tapes, audio recordings, no. 3, September 1955; Teletype, SAC Santoiana to Assistant Director Rosen, May 22, 1956, FBI 139-373-10.

64 King Tower tapes, audio recordings, nos. 3 and 4, September 1955.

65 King Tower tapes, audio recordings, no. 3, September 1955.

66 "Outline Summary Report Concerning Alleged Infractions of Rules and Regulations by Officials and Employees of the OLCC," Department of Justice/Attorney General Records, 61A-007, Oregon State Archives, Salem. Hereafter DOJ/AG Records.

67 Ibid.

68 King Tower tapes, audio recordings, no. 3, September 1955.

69 *Hearings*, 320.

70 Ibid.

71 King Tower tapes, audio recordings, no. 3, September 1955.

72 U.S. Congress, *McClellan Committee Hearings: 1957*, 16–19; *Hearings*, 320, 324.

73 King Tower tapes, audio recordings, no. 3, September 1955.

74 Abbott, *Portland*, 158; Lansing, *Portland*, 364.

75 Officer's Report, Oregon State Police, June 8, 1956.

76 Lansing, *Portland*, 367.

77 Qtd. in Lansing, *Portland*, 367.

78 Abbott, *Portland*, 163–64.

79 "E-R Commission Report on Activities during the year 1956," Fred Peterson Papers, City of Portland Stanley Parr Archives and Records Center, Portland, Oregon; *Hearings*, 15, 441.

80 "E-R Commission Report on Activities during the year 1956."

81 Officer's Report, Oregon State Police, May 15, 1956.

82 *Hearings*, 454.

83 Ibid.

84 Abbott, *Portland*, 164.

85 Tom Johnson, a former bootlegger, owned the Keystone Realty Company and used it to purchase profitable east side properties. He invested mostly in property in Portland's Williams Avenue district, especially nightclubs, and some properties catered to illegal activities. For example, according to journalist Phil Stanford, Johnson operated a gambling and after-hours club out of his Keystone Investment Company office on North Williams Avenue. Stanford, *Portland Confidential*, 86–89.

86 U.S Congress, *McClellan Committee Hearings: 1957*, 21; *Hearings*, 444.

87 *Hearings*, 113–14, 117.

88   Uris, "Trouble in River City," 195.
89   King Tower tapes, transcript, DOJ/AG Records; Officer's Report, Oregon State Police, July 2, 1956.
90   *Hearings*, 100, 134.

4. THE PORTLAND VICE SCANDAL

1   Wallace Turner was born in Titusville, Florida, in 1921, and earned a degree in journalism at the University of Missouri. He reported for the *Springfield* (Missouri) *Daily News* before moving to Portland in 1943, where he began reporting for the *Oregonian*. He left the *Oregonian* in 1960 to serve as news director for KPTV television in Portland and then moved to Washington, D.C., to serve as the assistant to the secretary of the U.S. Department of Health, Education, and Welfare. In 1962, he returned to newspaper reporting as a correspondent to the *New York Times* in San Francisco, where he served as bureau chief for fifteen years. As the Seattle bureau chief to the *New York Times*, Turner retired in 1988. He died September 18, 2010, in Springfield, Oregon. Brennan and Clarage, *Who's Who of Pulitzer Prize Winners*, 395; *San Francisco Chronicle*, September 22, 2010, C5.

2   William Lambert was born in Langford, South Dakota, in 1920. He was a reporter for the Oregon City *Banner-Courier* until 1950, when he went to work with Wallace Turner at the *Oregonian*. Shortly after the Portland vice scandal, Lambert left Portland for Washington, D.C., where he was first a television reporter and then a press agent. By the mid-1960s, he was a reporter for *Life* magazine and uncovered a bribery scandal that led to the resignation of Supreme Court Justice Abe Fortas. Lambert retired from reporting in 1985 and went to work as a consultant who helped to defend newspapers that were being sued for libel. Lambert died February 8, 1998. Agis Salpukas, "William Lambert, 78, Writer Who Exposed Justice Fortas," *New York Times*, February 16, 1998, A13; Brennan and Clarage, *Who's Who of Pulitzer Prize Winners*, 780.

3   Between April 13, 1956, and May 11, 1956, Wallace Turner and William Lambert wrote eleven articles in the exposé series. With these articles, dozens of other reports and editorials were written by the *Oregonian* staff and published between 1956 and 1960, as well as several articles in national magazines.

4   Turner interview.

5   Ibid.; Letter, Wallace Turner to author, December 11, 2004.

6   Turner interview.

7   *Time*, "Scandal in Portland," June 4, 1956, 81.

8   Letter, Wallace Turner to Arthur Kaplan, December 29, 2004, forwarded to author.

9   Ibid.

10   Turner interview.

11   Ibid.
12   *Oregonian*, April 19, 1956, 1.
13   Letter, Turner to Kaplan.
14   Qtd. in Uris, "Trouble in River City," 195.
15   Turner interview.
16   Ibid.
17   King Tower tapes, audio recordings, no. 2, n.d.
18   King Tower tapes, transcript, AKP, private collection.
19   King Tower tapes, audio recordings, no. 3, September 1955.
20   Oregon State Archives, "Governor Elmo Smith Biographical Notes."
      Available online at http://arcweb.sos.state.or.us/governors/Smith/
      smithoverview.html (accessed July 7, 2007).
21   Robert Thornton, "History of the Portland Vice Investigation,
      1953–1959," 16; DOJ/AG Records, Oregon State Archives, Salem.
22   *Oregonian*, April 19, 1956, 1.
23   Ibid.; *Oregonian*, April 21, 1956, 1.
24   *Oregonian*, April 21, 1956, 1.
25   Letter, Turner to author.
26   *Time*, April 8, 1957, 67.
27   *Oregonian*, April 20, 1956, 1.
28   Ibid.
29   Ibid.
30   *Oregon Journal*, April 20, 1956, 1. In a 1980 interview with Joseph Uris,
      William Langley insisted that he had written letters to Police Chief
      Purcell demanding that he close down the vice operations connected to
      Elkins. According to Langley, Chief Purcell took the letters to Elkins.
      Uris, "Trouble in River City," 196.
31   Ibid.
32   King Tower tapes, audio recordings, no. 2, n.d.; King Tower tapes,
      transcript, DOJ/AG Records.
33   Officer's Report, Oregon State Police, May 15, 1956; Stanford, *Portland
      Confidential*, 45–46.
34   King Tower tapes, audio recordings, no. 2, n.d.; King Tower tapes,
      transcript, DOJ/AG Records, August 22, 1955.
35   *Oregonian*, April 23, 1956, 1.
36   John Bardell Purcell served as Multnomah County sheriff from 1970
      to 1974. Linda McCarthy, "A History of Multnomah County Sher-
      iffs, mid-1800s to 1989," Oregon Sheriff's Association, 1992. Available
      online at http://www.co.multnomah.or.us/sheriff/history.htm (accessed
      August 1, 2005).
37   *State of Oregon v. William Langley, Thomas Maloney, Joseph McLaugh-
      lin*, February 14, 1957, Circuit Court of the State of Oregon for
      Multnomah County, Multnomah County Courthouse, Records, case
      nos. 34909, 34910, 34911; *Hearings*, 543; Officer's Report, Oregon State
      Police, June 8, 1956.

38 King Tower tapes, transcript, DOJ/AG Records, August 22, 1955.

39 Officer's Report, Oregon State Police, June 8, 1956.

40 Senate, *The McClellan Committee Hearings: 1957*, 21; *Hearings*, 553; *Oregonian*, April 23, 1956, 17.

41 Officer's Report, Oregon State Police, June 8, 1956.

42 Ibid.

43 Uris, "Trouble in River City," 211.

44 *Oregonian*, May 3, 1956, 1; *Time*, "Scandal in Portland," 81. The elisions are original to the *Oregonian* article. This portion of the King Tower tapes is missing.

45 Thornton, "History of the Portland Vice Investigation, 1953–1959," 7–8; Letter, Governor Elmo Smith to Attorney General Robert Thornton, April 23, 1956.

46 According to FBI documents, Governor Smith then contacted the Portland FBI office and "indicated his alarm over the recent attempt of the Teamsters to open up the city of Portland." Smith requested that the Bureau provide him with all information that FBI agents had collected on a number of individuals involved in the Portland vice scandal, including the Teamsters' West Coast Conference President Frank Brewster. By this time, the Seattle and Portland FBI offices had collected hundreds of pages of evidence on the Teamsters chief. FBI officials, however, did not provide the governor with any information regarding their investigation into labor racketeering, the Portland vice scandal, or municipal corruption. Correlation Summary, March 26, 1964, FBI 122-1812-18.

47 *Hearings*, 8; "Chronology of Illegal Search and Seizure of Materials, Clark Residence," AKP, private collection.

48 "Chronology of Illegal Search and Seizure of Materials, Clark Residence," AKP, private collection.

49 Ibid.

50 Ibid.

51 *State of Oregon v. William Langley, Brad Williams*, April 10, 1957, case no. 35173; *Raymond Clark and James Elkins v. George Minielly, Terry Schrunk, William Langley et al.*, April 13, 1957, case no. 34157; *State of Oregon v. Brad Williams*, April 15, 1957, case no. 35142; *State of Oregon v. Terry Schrunk*, April 15, 1957, case no. 35143; *State of Oregon v. Clyde Crosby*, April 19, 1957, case nos. 35168–35170; *Hearings*, 8.

52 Airtel, Portland SAC to Director, May 21, 1956, FBI 139-373-16.

53 *Raymond Clark and James Elkins v. George Minielly, Terry Schrunk, William Langley et al.*, April 13, 1957, case no. 34157; *State of Oregon v. Clyde Crosby*, April 19, 1957, case nos. 35168–35170; *Oregon Journal*, April 8, 1957, 1; "Chronology of Illegal Search and Seizure of Materials, Clark Residence," AKP, private collection.

54 Ibid.

55 Airtel, SAC Portland to Director, September 5, 1956, FBI 139-373-41.

56   Thornton, "History of the Portland Vice Investigation, 1953–1959," 10.
57   Ibid.
58   Turner interview.
59   *Oregonian*, June 5, 1956, 1.
60   Thornton, "History of the Portland Vice Investigation, 1953–1959," 17.
61   *Oregonian*, June 13, 1956, 1.
62   *Oregonian*, August 5, 1956, 1.
63   *State of Oregon v. Clyde Crosby*, April 19, 1956, case nos. 35168–35170;
      Oregonian, August 5, 1956, 1. Although there can be little doubt that
      Crosby feloniously conspired to profit from his position as a member of
      the Portland Exposition-Recreation Commission, his defenders made
      him out to be a victim rather than a criminal. At the twentieth annual
      session of the Western Conference of Teamsters in June 1956, the
      delegates passed a "resolution of confidence in International Represen-
      tative Clyde Crosby," which claimed that he was a "target of newspaper
      attacks." Shortly after the *Oregonian* exposé hit newsstands in April
      1956, Crosby filed a slander suit against the newspaper. *The Teamster*,
      August 1956, 14.
64   *Oregonian*, August 2, 1956, 1.
65   *State of Oregon v. William Langley, Thomas Maloney, and Joseph
      McLaughlin*, July 31, 1956, case no. 34316; *Oregonian*, August 5, 1956, 1.
66   *Oregonian*, August 2, 1956, 1.
67   Turner interview.
68   *Oregonian*, August 11, 1956, 1.
69   *State of Oregon v. James Purcell*, August 3, 1956, case no. 34334; *Orego-
      nian*, August 4, 1956, 1.
70   *Oregonian*, August 3, 1956, 1; *Oregonian*, August 5, 1956, 1.
71   Thornton, "History of the Portland Vice Investigation, 1953–1959," 16.

5. THE MCCLELLAN COMMITTEE

1   *Oregonian*, November 2, 1956, 1.
2   After the repeal of Prohibition in 1932, the Brewery Workers Union
     (BWU) reclaimed jurisdiction over the beer truck drivers in Wash-
     ington and Oregon. In May 1933, the American Federation of Labor
     (AFL) granted the Teamsters union jurisdiction over the drivers, but
     BWU officials refused to recognize the Teamsters' authority. The
     Teamsters, therefore, began a delivery boycott against what Dave Beck
     called "red label" beer—that is, beer brewed by BWU labor. While the
     boycott certainly affected the breweries, it was primarily directed at
     distributors and grocers, who were forced to support the union's inter-
     ests through threats of delivery interruptions. If a grocery stocked "red
     label" beer—such as Lucky Lager, Budweiser, Rainier, and Schlitz—
     then Teamsters' drivers were not allowed to deliver "white label"
     beer, i.e., beer not brewed by the BWU, to that store. Berner, *Seattle*

1921–1940, 359–60; Report, Portland SAC (unidentified) to Director, October 17, 1937, FBI 69-516-17.

3   Russell, *Out of the Jungle*, 113–15; Lichtenstein, *State of the Union*, 118.

4   Dubofsky, *State and Labor in Modern America*, 193, 195.

5   Ibid., 202, 204.

6   Lichtenstein, *State of the Union*, 115, 117. The AFL and CIO merged in 1955.

7   Theoharis and Cox, *Boss*, 10.

8   Theoharis, *From the Secret Files of J. Edgar Hoover*, 110.

9   Memo, FBI Executives' Conference to FBI Director, October 14, 1953, FBI 121-23278, reprinted in Theoharis, *From the Secret Files of J. Edgar Hoover*, 118.

10   Schrecker, *Many Are the Crimes*, 107.

11   Ibid., 141, 357.

12   Lichtenstein, *State of the Union*, 145.

13   "Third Interim Report of the Special Committee to Investigate Organized Crime in Interstate Commerce," reprinted in Gardner and Olson, eds., *Theft of the City*, 68–72.

14   Baltakis, "Agendas of Investigation," 16.

15   Kennedy, *Enemy Within*, 49–52.

16   Report, SAC Seattle, June 17, 1960, FBI 159-206, SE 159-4; Baltakis, "Agendas of Investigation," 15; Russell, *Out of the Jungle*, 174–75.

17   Baltakis, "Agendas of Investigation," 9–10; Kennedy, *Enemy Within*, 6.

18   Baltakis, "Agendas of Investigation," 11–12.

19   Murder, Incorporated, which operated from the 1920s until the 1940s, was a group of hit men, which included Charles "Lucky" Luciano, Meyer Lansky, Benjamin "Bugsy" Siegel, and Joe Adonis, that criminal syndicates hired to enforce mob edicts and protect criminal interests. Nash, *World Encyclopedia of Organized Crime*, 295.

20   Sheridan, *Fall and Rise of Jimmy Hoffa*, 17–19; Baltakis, "Agendas of Investigation," 11–12.

21   Sheridan, *Fall and Rise of Jimmy Hoffa*, 17–19; Baltakis, "Agendas of Investigation," 12–13.

22   Kennedy, *Enemy Within*, 7; Baltakis, "Agendas of Investigation," 13–14; Clark Mollenhoff, "The Teamsters Defy the Government," *Atlantic Monthly*, November 1958, 43–53.

23   In 1946 the Retail Clerks International Association organized a strike against Kahn's department store in Oakland, California; the action became a paralyzing general strike when the Merchants Association brought in nonunion truckers from Los Angeles. Because the retail clerks prevented an earlier attempt by the Teamsters to absorb their union, Beck and the Teamsters opposed the Retail Clerks union strike and sided with management rather than the workers. Persuasion was reinforced by intimidation when Beck and Teamsters leaders trucked in "goons" from Seattle, Detroit, Chicago, and St. Louis to physi-

cally intimidate those stubborn leaders of the Retail Clerks union. Newspaper reporters and the FBI believed that many of the "goons" were members of the Al Capone crime syndicate that was assisting the Teamsters union takeover of businesses and labor unions on the West Coast. In an interview by FBI agents in Los Angeles, one member of the Retail Clerks union claimed that he was followed home and beaten by a group of Teamsters' "goons" and then was contacted the following morning by the union, which wanted to know if he was ready to join. The violent dispute was finally brought to an end when the Retail Clerks International Association eventually signed a two-year contract with the Teamsters. Harrington, *Retail Clerks*, 73–75; Telegram, Hood to Rosen, May 20, 1949, FBI 6-128-3; Telegram, Hood to Rosen, June 2, 1949, FBI 6-128-7; Telegram, Hood to Director, September 21, 1949, FBI 6-128-18.

24 Telegram, Hood to Rosen, June 2, 1949, FBI 6-128-7; Kennedy, *Enemy Within*, 8.

25 Kennedy, *Enemy Within*, 9.

26 Mollenhoff, "The Teamsters Defy the Government," 47.

27 Kennedy, *Enemy Within*, 12.

28 *Oregonian*, December 6, 1956, 1; *Oregonian*, December 19, 1956, 1; Kennedy, *Enemy Within*, 255–62.

29 Kennedy, *Enemy Within*, 239.

30 Baltakis, "Agendas of Investigation," 15.

31 Report, Special Agent, Los Angeles, November 6, 1953, FBI 122-820-13; Report, Special Agent, Seattle, February 20, 1957, FBI 122-1403-18; Kennedy, *Enemy Within*, 10.

32 Kennedy, *Enemy Within*, 21–22.

33 *Oregonian*, February 18, 1957, 1.

34 *Oregonian*, February 16, 1957, 1; Kennedy, *Enemy Within*, 24.

35 Drukman, *Wayne Morse*, 103, 160–61. Senator Wayne Morse was a Republican from 1945 to 1952, became an Independent in 1952, and switched to the Democratic Party in 1955.

36 Turner interview.

37 *Oregonian*, February 16, 1957, 1.

38 *Hearings*, 6–7.

39 Ibid., 5–6.

40 Kennedy, *Enemy Within*, 261.

41 Mollenhoff, "The Teamsters Defy the Government," 50.

42 *Interim Report*, 39.

43 *Hearings*, 80, 104.

44 *Oregonian*, March 6, 1957, 1.

45 *Interim Report*, 33.

46 *Oregonian*, March 7, 1957, 1.

47 Turner interview.

48 Kennedy, *Enemy Within*, 262.

49   *Hearings*, 934–37.

50   Ibid., 49.

51   Ibid., 61.

52   *Interim Report*, 33–34.

53   Ibid., 30; *Oregonian*, March 8, 1957, 1; *Oregonian*, March 29, 1957, 1.

54   *Hearings*, 573, 577; *Oregonian*, March 8, 1957, 1.

55   *Hearings*, 573, 577, 585, 593; *Oregonian*, March 8, 1957, 1.

56   *Hearings*, 564, 579; *Oregonian*, March 8, 1957, 1.

57   *Hearings*, 564; *Oregonian*, March 8, 1957, 1.

58   Lansing, *Portland*, 373.

59   Officer's Report, Oregon State Police, May 14, 1956.

60   King Tower tapes, transcript, August 22, 1955; Officer's Report, Oregon State Police, May 14, 1956; Officer's Report, Oregon State Police, July 2, 1956.

61   In his record of these court proceedings, Attorney General Robert Thornton does not reveal his new evidence.

62   Coincidentally, before the test, the sheriff asked Thornton if he could have his photo taken with the polygraph machine and the test administrators, "a publicity stunt," the attorney general later recalled, and an attempt to make light of the charges during the mayoral campaign. When Thornton denied the request, Schrunk arranged for a photo of himself and Multnomah County's polygraph machine to be printed in the local newspapers. *Oregonian*, November 3, 1956, 1; Thornton, "History of the Portland Vice Investigation," 19, 26.

63   Officer's Report, Oregon State Police, July 24, 1956.

64   Multnomah County commissioners appointed Terry Schrunk to the sheriff post in 1948 in response, journalist Phil Stanford asserts, to pressure from local Teamsters union officials. Stanford maintains that the Teamsters paid each county commissioner $10,000 to appoint Schrunk. At that time, Schrunk was a captain in the Portland Fire Bureau and was the Northwest representative of the Firemen's Union. *Portland Tribune*, August 23, 2002, C6; Turner interview.

65   *Hearings*, 90.

66   Mary V. Tobkin, interview by Linda Brody, SC9661, tape recording 979.111T6298 B1981, February 6, 1981, OHSRL, Portland.

67   Uris, "Trouble in River City," 211.

68   *Oregonian*, November 8, 1956, 1.

69   *Oregonian*, March 30, 1957, 1.

70   Turner interview; Sidney Lezak, interview with author, November 19, 2002.

71   *Oregonian*, March 30, 1957, 1.

72   *Interim Report*, 32.

73   Ibid.

74   *Hearings*, 653–54; *Interim Report*, 32.

75   *Interim Report*, 33.

76 Ibid.
77 *Oregonian*, March 29, 1957, 1.
78 U.S. Department of Labor, Office of Compliance Assistance Policy,
    Labor-Management Reporting and Disclosure Act of 1959. Avail-
    able online at http://www.dol.gov/compliance/laws/comp-lmrda.htm
    (accessed September 29, 2010; Lichtenstein, *State of the Union*, 164;
    Dubofsky, *State and Labor in Modern America*, 218; Baltakis, "Agendas
    of Investigation," 415.
79 Jacobs, *Mobsters, Unions, and Feds*, 15.
80 Baltakis, "Agendas of Investigation," 409.
81 Lichtenstein, *State of the Union*, 162–63.
82 James and James, *Hoffa and the Teamsters*, 22.
83 Kennedy, *Enemy Within*, 320. From the 1930s until his disappearance
    in 1975, Detroit Teamster Jimmy Hoffa had numerous legal troubles.
    In 1957, Hoffa was arrested on federal charges for attempting to bribe
    a McClellan Committee investigator. In March 1964, when he was
    Teamsters union president, Hoffa was convicted of jury tampering,
    and in July 1964, he was found guilty of conspiracy and mail and wire
    fraud. Russell, *Out of the Jungle*, 222–23.
84 Kennedy, *Enemy Within*, 320. Though he never held political office,
    Beck commanded considerable political influence in Washington
    State. According to a March 1957 FBI report to the McClellan Com-
    mittee, Seattle's mayor had provided Beck police protection in the
    1930s and the Teamsters' chief influenced the appointment of the city's
    police chief in 1941. The Teamsters union president also served on the
    board of regents at the University of Washington and was a panelist
    on the Washington State Board of Pardons. Letter, Deputy Attorney
    General William Rogers to Director Hoover, March 21, 1957, FBI
    62-100749-30; Report, Los Angeles SAC to Director, August 11, 1949,
    FBI 6-128-14; Memo, A. Rosen to Mr. Ladd, December 27, 1957, FBI
    58-2242-5; Washington Capital News Service, April 11, 1961, FBI 122-
    1403-11-H.
85 *Interim Report*, 61.
86 *Frank Brewster, Appellant, v. United States of America, Appellee*, case no.
    14145, United States Court of Appeals, District of Columbia Circuit,
    February 20, 1958; *The International Teamster*, May 1958, 8.
87 *Hearings*, 939.

EPILOGUE: THE FALLOUT

1 *Oregon Journal*, March 29, 1957, 1.
2 Turner interview.
3 *Oregonian*, June 20, 1957, 1; *Oregonian*, June 21, 1957, 1; Officer's
   Report, Oregon State Police, May 8, 1956; Officer's Report, Oregon
   State Police, May 14, 1956.

4   *Oregonian*, June 27, 1957, 1.

5   Turner interview.

6   J. C. Ross to Senator John L. McClellan, January 19, 1957, JMP, Special Collections, Riley-Hickingbotham Library, OBU, Arkadelphia, Arkansas.

7   Percy Murray to Senator John L. McClellan, January 30, 1957, JMP, OBU.

8   Lee McCord to Senator John McClellan, April 29, 1957, JMP, OBU.

9   Baltakis, "Agendas of Investigation," 412.

10   Wallace Turner to Arthur Kaplan, December 29, 2004.

11   Amil Spada, interview with author, October 8, 2002.

12   Mr. Hughes to Senator John McClellan, March 9, 1957, JMP, OBU.

13   C. L. Aydelott et al. to Sen. John McClellan, March 7, 1957, JMP, OBU.

14   Correspondence, "Derogatory File," JMP, OBU.

15   *Oregonian*, June 29, 1957, 1.

16   Swarthout, "The 1960 Election in Oregon," 356–59.

17   Ibid., 359.

18   Wes Barthelmes, interview with Roberta W. Greene, May 20, 1969, transcript, Robert F. Kennedy Papers, John F. Kennedy Library, Boston, Massachusetts.

19   Turner interview.

20   Uris, "Trouble in River City," 204.

21   Abbott, *Portland*, 170.

22   Thornton, "History of the Portland Vice Investigation, 1953–1959," 9–10.

23   Turner interview.

24   Letter, Arthur Kaplan to Robert Thornton, May 18, 1957, AKP, private collection; *Capital Journal*, October 19, 1957, 1, AKP, private collection.

25   Letter, Arthur Kaplan to Robert Thornton, May 18, 1957, AKP, private collection.

26   Thornton, "History of the Portland Vice Investigation, 1953–1959," 12, 25.

27   *Oregonian*, September 25, 1957, 1.

28   Thornton, "History of the Portland Vice Investigation, 1953–1959," 16.

29   Uris, "Trouble in River City," 195.

30   *Oregon Journal*, April 8, 1957, 1.

31   *Oregon Journal*, April 9, 1957, 1.

32   *Oregon Journal*, April 10, 1957, 1.

33   *Oregonian*, October 7, 1957, 14.

34   *Oregonian*, September 25, 1957, 14.

35   Ibid.

36   Turner interview.

37   *Oregonian*, September 25, 1957, 14.

38   *Oregon Journal*, March 7, 1960, 27; *Oregon Journal*, March 29, 1960, 6;

Oregonian, March 8, 1960, 27; *Oregonian*, March 29, 1960, 14; *Oregonian*, March 30, 1960, 6.

39 Thornton, "History of the Portland Vice Investigation, 1953–1959," 9–10.

40 Turner interview.

41 Kennedy, *Enemy Within*, 256.

42 Ibid.

43 Turner interview.

44 Memo, SAC Portland to Director, April 18, 1961, FBI 139-373-254.

45 Turner interview.

46 *James Butler Elkins and Raymond Frederick Clark v. United States*, U.S. Supreme Court, 126 U.S. 1669 (1960); see also *Oregon Journal*, March 7, 1960, 27; *Oregon Journal*, March 29, 1960, 6; *Oregonian*, March 8, 1960, 27; *Oregonian*, March 29, 1960, 14; *Oregonian*, March 30, 1960, 6; Turner interview.

47 Lezak interview. Lezak was U.S. Attorney for Oregon from 1961 to 1982, initially appointed by Kennedy for his party affiliation and his earlier legal attack on the Teamsters. In 1959, as lawyer for the Office Employees Local 11, Lezak sued the Western Conference of Teamsters for unfair labor practices. The Oregon Supreme Court later ruled that the Teamsters were guilty of forcing their own office employees to join the union.

48 Memo, SAC Portland to Director, September 26, 1961, FBI 139-373-262.

49 Kennedy, *Enemy Within*, 260–61.

50 Conversation transcript, Colleen and James Elkins with Arthur Kaplan, November 25, 1959, AKP, private collection.

51 *Oregonian*, November 7, 1959, 1.

52 Lezak interview.

53 *Oregon Journal*, October 10, 1968, 1; *Oregonian*, October 11, 1968, 1.

54 Stanford, *Portland Confidential*, 187.

55 Thornton, "History of the Portland Vice Investigation, 1953–1959," 27.

56 Chuck Bollinger, interview with author, June 14, 2002. In the mid-1970s, Bollinger and the Portland Police Bureau's Intelligence Division investigated Seattle's Colacurcio crime family.

57 Thornton, "History of the Portland Vice Investigation, 1953–1959," 27.

58 Bollinger interview.

59 Moose, *Three Weeks in October*, 96.

60 Turner interview.

BIBLIOGRAPHY

Abbott, Carl. *Portland: Planning, Politics, and Growth in a Twentieth-Century City.* Lincoln: University of Nebraska Press, 1983.

Ackerman, Susan-Rose. *Corruption and Government: Causes, Consequences, and Reform.* New York: Cambridge University Press, 1999.

Alexander, Herbert E., and Gerald E. Caiden, eds. *The Politics and Economics of Organized Crime.* Lexington, MA: D. C. Heath and Company, 1985.

Allman, Joseph M. "The 1968 Elections in Oregon." *The Western Political Quarterly* 14 (March 1961): 355–64.

Atlantic Monthly. November 1958.

Auerbach, Jerold S. *Labor and Liberty: The La Follette Committee and the New Deal.* Indianapolis, IN: The Bobbs-Merrill Company, Inc., 1966.

Baltakis, Anthony V. "Agendas of Investigation: The McClellan Committee, 1957–1958." PhD diss., University of Akron, 1997.

Barthelmes, Wes. Interview with Roberta W. Greene, May 20, 1969. Transcript, Robert F. Kennedy Papers, John F. Kennedy Library, Boston, MA.

Bean, Walton. *Boss Ruef's San Francisco: The Story of the Union Labor Party, Big Business, and the Graft Prosecution.* Berkeley: University of California Press, 1952.

Bell, Daniel. *The End of Ideology.* Glencoe, IL: The Free Press, 1960.

Berman, David R., and Bruce D. Merrill. "Citizens Attitudes toward Municipal Reform Institutions: A Testing of Some Assumptions." *The Western Political Quarterly* 29 (June 1976): 274–83.

Berner, Richard C. *Seattle 1900–1920: From Boomtown, Urban Turbulence, to Restoration.* Seattle, WA: Charles Press, 1991.

———. *Seattle 1921–1940: From Boom to Bust.* Seattle, WA: Charles Press, 1992.

———. *Seattle Transformed: World War II to Cold War.* Seattle, WA: Charles Press, 1999.
Bodnar, John, Roger Simon, and Michael P. Weber. *Lives of Their Own: Blacks, Italians, and Poles in Pittsburgh, 1900–1960.* Urbana: University of Illinois Press, 1982.
Bollinger, Chuck. Interview with author. June 14, 2002. Clackamas, Oregon.
Brennan, Elizabeth, and Elizabeth C. Clarage. *Who's Who of Pulitzer Prize Winners.* Phoenix: Oryx Press, 1999.
Brill, Steven. *The Teamsters.* New York: Simon and Schuster, 1978.
Bureau of Municipal Research. *Organization and Business Methods of the City Government of Portland, Oregon.* New York: Bureau of Municipal Research, 1913.
Chambliss, William. *On the Take: From Petty Crooks to Presidents.* Bloomington: Indiana University Press, 1978.
Chin, Gabriel J., ed. *New York City Police Corruption Investigation Commissions, 1894–1994.* Buffalo, NY: William S. Hein and Co., Inc., 1997.
City Club of Portland Bulletin. January 1945–February 1948.
Clement, Elizabeth Alice. *Love For Sale: Courting, Treating, and Prostitution in New York City, 1900–1945.* Chapel Hill: University of North Carolina Press, 2006.
DeMarco, Gordon. *A Short History of Portland.* San Francisco, CA: Lexikos, 1990.
Drukman, Mason. *Wayne Morse: A Political Biography.* Portland: Oregon Historical Society Press, 1997.
Dubofsky, Melvyn. *The State and Labor in Modern America.* Chapel Hill: University of North Carolina Press, 1994.
Dunlop, M. H. *Gilded City: Scandal and Sensation in Turn-of-the-Century New York.* New York: William Morrow, 2000.
Eisenstadt, Abraham S., Ari Hoogenboom, and Hans L. Trefousse, eds. *Before Watergate: Problems of Corruption in American Society.* Brooklyn, NY: Brooklyn College Press, 1977.
Gardiner, John A. *The Politics of Corruption: Organized Crime in an American City.* New York: Russell Sage Foundation, 1970.
Gardiner, John A., and David J. Olson, eds. *Theft of the City: Readings on Corruption in Urban America.* Bloomington: Indiana University Press, 1974.
Garnel, Donald. *The Rise of Teamster Power in the West.* Berkeley: University of California Press, 1972.
Goldwater, Barry. Papers. Arizona Historical Foundation, Hayden Library, Arizona State University, Tempe.
Haller, Mark H. "Urban Crime and Criminal Justice: The Chicago Case." *The Journal of American History* 57 (December 1970): 619–35.
Hammack, David C. "Problems in the Historical Study of Power in the Cities and Towns of the United States, 1800–1960." *The American Historical Review* 83 (April 1978): 323–49.

Harrington, Michael. *The Retail Clerks*. New York: John Wiley and Sons, Inc., 1962.

Hays, Samuel P. "The Politics of Reform in Municipal Government in the Progressive Era." *Pacific Northwest Quarterly* 55 (October 1964): 157–69.

Heidenheimer, Arnold J., Michael Johnston, and Victor T. LeVine. *Political Corruption: A Handbook*. New Brunswick, NJ: Transaction Publishers, 1989.

Hofstadter, Richard. *The Age of Reform: From Bryan to F.D.R.* New York: Vintage Books, 1955.

The International Teamster. April 1957–October 1958.

Jacobs, James B. *Mobsters, Unions, and Feds: The Mafia and the American Labor Movement*. New York: New York University Press, 2006.

James, Ralph C., and Estelle Dinerstein James. *Hoffa and the Teamsters: A Study of Union Power*. Princeton, NJ: D. Van Nostrand Company, Inc., 1965.

Johnston, Robert D. *The Radical Middle Class: Populist Democracy and the Question of Capitalism in Progressive Era Portland, Oregon*. Princeton, NJ: Princeton University Press, 2003.

Kaplan, Arthur. Papers. Private collection.

Kennedy, Robert F. *The Enemy Within*. New York: Harper & Brothers, 1960.

———. Papers, John F. Kennedy Library, Boston, MA.

King, Harry. *Box Man: A Professional Thief's Journey*. New York: Harper and Row Publishers, 1972.

King Tower Tapes. Audio Recordings. 1955 copy. Collection of the author.

———. Transcripts, Department of Justice/Attorney General Records. 61A-007. Oregon State Archives, Salem.

Kolko, Gabriel. *The Triumph of Conservatism: A Reinterpretation of American History, 1900–1916*. New York: The Free Press, 1963.

Lansing, Jewell. *Portland: People, Politics, and Power, 1851–2001*. Corvallis: Oregon State University Press, 2003.

Law Library of Congress. "American Women: Immigration." Available online at http://memory.loc.gov/ammem/awhhtml/awlaw3/immigration. html (accessed October 3, 2010).

Lee, Dorothy McCullough. Papers. OHSRL, Portland.

Leeson, Fred. *Rose City Justice: A Legal History of Portland, Oregon*. Portland: Oregon Historical Society Press, 1998.

Lezak, Sidney. Interview with author. November 19, 2002. Portland, Oregon.

Lichtenstein, Nelson. *State of the Union: A Century of American Labor*. Princeton, NJ: Princeton University Press, 2002.

Lucia, Ellis. *The Conscience of a City: Fifty Years of City Club Service in Portland*. Portland, OR: The City Club of Portland, 1966.

MacColl, E. Kimbark. *The Growth of a City: Power and Politics in Portland, Oregon, 1915–1950*. Portland: The Georgian Press, 1979.

———. *Merchants, Money, and Power: The Portland Establishment, 1843–1913*. Portland: The Georgian Press, 1988.

————. *The Shaping of a City: Business and Politics in Portland, Oregon, 1885–1915.* Portland: The Georgian Press, 1976.

Malloy, Thomas. Interview with Adam Hodges. Transcript, OHSRL, Portland.

Marsh, Floyd R. *20 Years a Soldier of Fortune.* Portland: Binford & Mort, 1976.

McCallum, John D. *Dave Beck.* Vancouver, B.C.: Gordon Soules Book Publishers, 1978.

McCarthy, Linda. "A History of Multnomah County Sheriffs, mid-1800s to 1989." Oregon Sheriff's Association, 1992. Available online at http://www.co.multnomah.or.us/sheriff/history.htm (accessed August 1, 2005).

McClellan, John L. Papers. Special Collections, Riley-Hickingbotham Library, Ouachita Baptist University, Arkadelphia, AR.

McCormick, Richard L. "The Discovery That Business Corrupts Politics: A Reappraisal of the Origins of Progressivism." *The American Historical Review* 86 (April 1981): 247–74.

Miller, Zane L. "Boss Cox's Cincinnati: A Study in Urbanization and Politics, 1880–1914." *The Journal of American History* 54 (March 1968): 823–38.

Monkkonen, Eric H. *America Becomes Urban: The Development of U.S. Cities and Towns, 1780–1980.* Berkeley: University of California Press, 1988.

Moose, Charles. *Three Weeks in October: The Manhunt for the Serial Sniper.* New York: Dutton Books, 2003.

Mullins, William H. *The Depression and the Urban West Coast, 1929–1933.* Bloomington: Indiana University Press, 1991.

Multnomah County Courthouse. Criminal Case Records, April 1956–January 1959. Circuit Court of the State of Oregon for Multnomah County, Portland.

Myers, Gloria E. *A Municipal Mother: Portland's Lola Baldwin, America's First Policewoman.* Corvallis: Oregon State University Press, 1995.

Nash, Jay R. *World Encyclopedia of Organized Crime.* New York: Da Capo Press, 1993.

New York Journal-American. September 1956.

Oregonian. August 1912 –October 1968.

Oregon Journal. January 1906–October 1968.

Oregon State Police Records. Officers' Reports, 1956.

Perkins, Hayes. "Here and There: Volume I." Unpublished manuscript October 1898, OHSRL, Portland.

Peterson, Fred. Papers. City of Portland Stanley Parr Archives and Record Center, Portland, Oregon.

Pitzer, Paul C. "Dorothy McCullough Lee: The Successes and Failures of 'Dottie-Do-Good.'" *Oregon Historical Quarterly* 91 (Spring 1990): 5–42.

Portland City Council Minutes. April 1951–December 1955. City of Portland Stanley Parr Archives and Records Center, Portland, Oregon.

Portland Tribune. April 2001–August 2002.

Reckless, Walter C. "The Impact of War on Crime, Delinquency, and Prostitution." *The American Journal of Sociology* 48 (November 1942): 378–86.

Reed, Thomas Harrison. *Municipal Government in the United States.* New York: The Century Co., 1926.

Riley, Earl. Papers. OHSRL, Portland.

Riordon, William L. *Plunkitt of Tammany Hall: A Series of Very Plain Talks on Very Practical Politics, Delivered by Ex-Senator George Washington Plunkitt, the Tammany Philosopher, from His Rostrum—the New York County Court-House Bootblack Stand.* New York: Alfred A. Knopf, 1948.

Russell, Thaddeus. *Out of the Jungle: Jimmy Hoffa and the Remaking of the American Working Class.* New York: Alfred A. Knopf, 2001.

Schrecker, Ellen. *Many Are the Crimes: McCarthyism in America.* Boston: Little, Brown and Company, 1998.

Schwantes, Carlos A. *The Pacific Northwest: An Interpretative History.* Lincoln: University of Nebraska Press, 1989.

Seattle Intelligencer. April–May 1957.

Seattle Times. November 1996- June 2008.

Sheridan, Walter. *The Fall and Rise of Jimmy Hoffa.* New York: Saturday Review Press, 1972.

Spada, Amil. Interview with author. July–October 2002. Portland, Oregon.

Stanford, Phil. *Portland Confidential: Sex, Crime, and Corruption in the Rose City.* Portland: WestWinds Press, 2004.

Steffens, Lincoln. *The Shame of the Cities.* New York: McClure, Phillips, and Co., 1904.

Swarthout, John M. "The 1960 Election in Oregon." *The Western Political Quarterly* 14 (March 1961): 355–64.

Talbot, Henry Russell. *Report of the Portland Vice Commission to the Mayor of the City of Portland, Oregon, January 1913: The same being a compilation of all the reports made by the Commission on various phases of what is commonly known as the "Social Evil."* Portland: Portland Vice Commission, 1913.

Teaford, Jon C. *Cities of the Heartland: The Rise and Fall of the Industrial Midwest.* Bloomington: Indiana University Press, 1993.

———. "'King Richard' Hatcher: Mayor of Gary." *Journal of Negro History* 77 (Summer 1992): 126–40.

The Teamster. May 1956–December 1958.

Terry, Stanley. Interview by Linda Brody, 1982. Transcript, Stanley Terry Oral History Collection, OHSRL, Portland.

Thelen, David P. "Social Tensions and the Origins of Progressivism." *Journal of American History* 56 (September 1969): 323–41.

Theoharis, Athan G., ed. *The FBI: A Comprehensive Reference Guide.* New York: The Oryx Press, 2000.

———. *From the Secret Files of J. Edgar Hoover.* Chicago: Ivan R. Dee, 1991.

Theoharis, Athan G., and John Stuart Cox. *The Boss: J. Edgar Hoover and the Great American Inquisition.* Philadelphia: Temple University Press, 1988.

Thornton, Robert. "History of the Portland Vice Investigation, 1953–1959." Unpublished Manuscript, June 1959. Department of Justice/Attorney General Records, 61A-007. Oregon State Archives, Salem.

Time. June 5, 1956–April 8, 1957.

Tobkin, Mary V. Interview with Linda Brody. Tape recording, OHSRL, Portland.

Turner, Wallace. Interview with author, August 5, 2003. Seattle, Washington.

Uris, Joseph. "Trouble in River City: An Analysis of an Urban Vice Probe." PhD diss., Portland State University, 1981.

U.S. Congress. Senate. *The McClellan Committee Hearings: 1957.* Washington, D.C.: Bureau of National Affairs, 1958.

U.S. Congress. Senate. Select Committee on Improper Activities in the Labor or Management Field. *Hearings Before the Select Committee on Improper Activities in the Labor or Management Field.* 85th Cong., 1st sess. (February–March 1957). Parts 1–4.

U.S. Congress. Senate. Select Committee on Improper Activities in the Labor or Management Field. *Interim Report of the Senate Select Committee on Improper Activities in the Labor or Management Field.* 85th Cong., 2nd sess., 1958. S. Rep. 1417.

U.S. Department of Commerce. Bureau of the Census. "Wartime Changes in Population and Family Characteristics: Portland-Vancouver Production Area." Series CA-2, no. 6. Washington, D.C.: U.S. Department of Commerce, 1944.

U.S. Department of Justice. Federal Bureau of Investigation. David D. Beck. 1939–1961, FBI 6-128, 58-2242, 60-2838, 62-100749, 69-516, 72-1052, 73-17658, 92-136, 92-2423, 122-820, 122-1403, 122-1812-18, 122-2152, vol. 1–4 and sub A.

U.S. Department of Justice. Federal Bureau of Investigation. Frank Brewster. 1955–1964, FBI 122-1812, 122-HQ-2100-159 to 122-HQ-2111-206, and sub A.

U.S. Department of Justice. Federal Bureau of Investigation. James Elkins. 1956–1960, FBI 139-373-156 to 139-373-240.

U.S. National Archives. "Description of the records of the Subcommittee Investigating Violations of Free Speech and Labor, 1936–1941." Chapter 14.19, 74th Cong. Available online at http://www.archives.gov/records_of_congress/Senate_guide/Chapter_14.html (accessed October 3, 2010).

Vollmer, August. "Portland Bureau Survey." August 1947. OHSRL, Portland.

Warner, Sam Bass, Jr. "If All the World Were Philadelphia: A Scaffolding for Urban History, 1774–1930." *The American Historical Review* 74 (October 1968): 26–43.

Wong, Marie Rose. *Sweet Cakes, Long Journey: The Chinatowns of Portland, Oregon.* Seattle: University of Washington Press, 2004.

Yoles, Melanie A. "Committee of Fourteen Records, 1905–1932." New York Public Library, Manuscripts and Archives Division, May 1985, rev. July 2000. Available online at http://legacy.www.nypl.org/research/chss/spe/rbk/faids/commfour.pdf (accessed October 3, 2010).

INDEX

Page numbers in italics refer to photos.

156–59; and McClellan Committee investigation, 4, 14, 119, 124–32; and Oregon politics, 148–49; political agenda of, 147; in Portland, 128–29, 146–47; in Seattle, 128; and Terry Schrunk, 146–47, 149; and William Langley, 134

Keystone Realty Company, 175n85

King, Harry, 60, 61–62, 63, 72, 159, 171n87

King Tower apartments, 20, 89, 91, 133, 159, 165n18

King Tower tapes, 96, 152; confiscation of, 110–12, 155; creation of, 89–90, 133, 155–56, 159, 165n15; given to the *Oregonian*, 99–100, 102, 178n44; and grand jury investigation, 14, 90–91, 110, 112–13; and McClellan Committee, 133–34; transcripts from, 103–4, 107, 18, 136–37

Kinnicutt, Mrs. Eugene, 55

Knotty Pine Tavern, 91

KPOJ, 111

labor racketeering: in Cleveland, 124; in Detroit, 74, 97, 129; and Jimmy Hoffa, 76–77, 124–25, 126–27, 129; in Los Angeles, 127–28, 129; in New York, 97, 123, 126–27, 129; in Portland, 4, 11, 13, 73, 74–75, 77, 80–84, 85, 86–90, 99–100, 104–5, 113–14, 119, 128–29, 131–32, 143, 152, 160–61, 162; in Seattle, 8, 74; and Teamsters union, 3–5, 12–13, 73, 74–75, 76–77, 78, 79, 97–98; and U.S. Senate Subcommittee on Investigations, 3–4, 13–14, 116, 119, 130

Ladd, Charles, 35

LaFortune, Robert, 115

LaGuardia, Fiorello, 47, 168n2. *See also* New York

Lambert, William, 24; biography of, 176n2; and Heywood Broun Award, 105, 153–54; and King Tower tapes, 96, 99–100, 102, 152;

and McClellan Committee, 4, 131–32, 143; and the *Oregonian*, 3, 12, 74, 101, 104–5, 109, 113, 128, 176n3; and Wayne Morse, 131

Lampert, L. J., 70

Landes, Bertha, 8, 47, 167n2. *See also* Seattle

Landrum-Griffin Act, 142

Lane, Harry, 7, 37–39, 45

Langley, William, 19, 102, 114–15, 147, 151, 152–53, 156, 172n105; assault on Allan DeLay, 115; biography of, 85–86; and the China Lantern, 86, 132–33; conviction of, 152; and elections, 73, 85, 86, 106, 109, 129, 133, 138; indictment of, 100, 113, 114; and James Elkins, 73, 86, 90, 96, 97, 106–7, 132–33, 136–37, 152; and James Purcell, 108, 177n30; and King Tower tapes, 14, 73, 90–91, 96, 99–100, 103–4, 105, 110, 111–12, 133–34, 136–37, 152, 156; and McClellan Committee, 131, 134, 143–44; and *Oregon Journal*, 106–7, 154; and Oregon Liquor Control Commission investigation, 14, 89, 90–91, 92, 133, 152; and Teamsters union, 85, 86–87, 99–100, 105, 106, 108, 129, 133, 138

Lansing, Jewell, 14–15

Lansky, Meyer, 180n19

Laundry and Dye Works Drivers Union, 77

law enforcement corruption: in Chicago, 9, 10, 97; in Detroit, 97; in New York, 10, 97, 160; in Philadelphia, 123; in Portland, 10, 12, 32–34, 42, 44, 45, 47–48, 51, 55, 59, 62–64, 70–71, 73–74, 85, 86–87, 91, 99–100, 103, 115, 132, 135–36, 137–42, 145, 151, 152, 153, 161, 162

Lawrence, David, 47, 168n2

Lee, Dorothy McCullough, 17, 47, 169n45, 171n100; and Charles Pray, 66, 69; early career of, 65; and elections, 65–66, 69, 93; criticism of, 68, 69; recall effort against, 69; reform efforts of, 66,

Toledo, OH, 7
Torrio, Johnny, 28
Travelers Insurance Company, 49
Triscaro, Louis, 124
Truman, Harry, 120
Tubber, Gideon, 8
Tucker, Raymond, 47, 167n2. *See also*
St. Louis
Turf Club, 170n46
Turner, Wallace, 24, 109, 113, 162;
biography of, 176n1; and Heywood Broun Award, 105, 153–54;
and James Elkins, 62, 99–101,
102, 132, 153, 155–59, 161; and
King Tower tapes, 99, 102, 103,
110, 133–34, 159; and McClellan
Committee, 4, 131–32, 143; and
Mike Elliot, 67; and *Oregonian*
exposé, 3, 12, 74, 99–100, 102,
104–6, 128–29, 143, 147, 153, 155,
176n3; and Robert Kennedy, 119,
128, 146–47, 149, 157–58; and
Robert Thornton, 150; and Terry
Schrunk, 139, 146–47, 149; and
Wayne Morse, 131; and William
Langley, 115, 133–34, 147
Tweed, William M., 28

Unauthorized Publication or Use of
Communications Statute, 157
Union Casualty Life Insurance
Agency, 125
United Auto Workers, 120, 122
United Mine Workers, 120, 122
Uris, Joseph, 15, 109, 138, 150, 177n30
U.S. Congress Joint Committee of
Government Operations, 125
U.S. House Government Operations
Subcommittee on Investigations,
124
U.S. Maritime Commission, 49
U.S. National Bank, 41
U.S. Senate Committee on Government Operations, 125, 127, 130, 143
U.S. Senate Committee on Labor
and Public Welfare, 122
U.S. Senate Select Committee
on Improper Activities in the

Labor or Management Field. *See*
McClellan Committee
U.S. Senate Special Committee on
Organized Crime and Interstate
Commerce. *See* Kefauver Committee
U.S. Senate Subcommittee on
Investigations: and Communism,
121–122; and labor racketeering, 3–4, 13–14, 116, 119, 130; and
municipal corruption, 58; and
organized crime in Portland, 60,
61, 116; and Portland politics, 116;
and Portland vice scandal, 98,
118–19
U.S. Senate Subcommittee on Labor
Management Relations, 122

Vance, John, 135–36
Vancouver, B.C., 78
Vanport, 50–51
venereal disease, 52–53
Vice Commission of 1912, viii, 40–41,
45
Villard, Henry, 32
Vollmer, August, 55, 56
Vollmer Report, 55–56, 64, 65

Wagner Act, 119, 120–21
Walkins, W. H., 27
Wallen, Elmer, 146
Weinhard, Henry, 33, 34, 41
West, Oswald, 41
Western Conference of Teamsters,
78, 79, 80, 128, 140, 143, 179n63,
185n47
Willamette Iron and Steel, 49
Williams, Brad, 90, 110, 155
Williams, George, 38
Williamson, John, 31
Winter, Al, 58, 66, 136, 137, 169n46
Woodward, Bob, 106
Wright, Budge, 83
Wycoff, Ralph, 151

Zeidler, Frank, 47, 167n2
Zenith Rooms, 53
Zusman, Nate, 60, 62